DOES SHE . . .
OR DOESN'T SHE?

DOES SHE . . .
OR DOESN'T SHE?

And How She Did It

Shirley Polykoff

DOUBLEDAY & COMPANY, INC.
Garden City, New York
1975

The author gratefully acknowledges the co-operation of Clairol Incorporated in permitting the use throughout the text of the following trademarks owned by Clairol Incorporated or its related companies: *Does She . . . Or Doesn't She?*; *Loving Care*; *Is It True Blondes Have More Fun?*; *The Closer He Gets the Better You Look*; *She Still Does!*; *Miss Clairol*; *Bufferin*; *Hair Color So Natural Only Her Hairdresser Knows for Sure*; *Hate That Gray? Wash It Away! Colors Only the Gray Without Changing Your Natural Hair Color*; *Lady Clairol*; *Kindness*; *Nice 'N Easy*; *Silk & Silver*; *Ultra-Blue*.

Library of Congress Cataloging in Publication Data

Polykoff, Shirley.
   Does she . . . or doesn't she?

   1. Polykoff, Shirley. 2. Advertising—United States. I. Title.
HF5810.P65A35   659.1′092′4 [B]
ISBN 0-385-06167-6
Library of Congress Catalog Card Number 74–18824

For my daughters,
Alix Nelson and *Laurie Zucker*

Contents

DOES SHE . . .
OR DOESN'T SHE?

1

The American Dreamboat

Does she . . . or doesn't she?

I do.

I do it blonde. A discreet mixture of Fresh Honey and Innocent Ivory. And I have more fun—even though it seems to me I'm always seven pounds over the perfect weight prescribed for women five feet five and a half with medium bone structure.

So I'm always on a diet. My husband, George, used to say it was easy to tell when I was eating something delicious. I looked so miserable.

Next year—it's always next year—I'll be older than God. This year I feel younger than springtime. So I can identify with every age group. Identifying is very vital in the advertising business. But that's easy for me because I've been just about everything a woman can be. Except maybe a bitch. Though I've been called that too.

I've been a virgin, a sweetheart, a wife, a mother, a grandmother, a mistress, in that order, and I've savored each role. I've been a career girl, a junior V.P., a senior V.P., a member of the board, a president. And a widow too long. But I've never been a boy. And that's what my mother wanted.

I was brought up to believe that the best thing that could happen to a girl was to grow up to become a mother. Provided, of course, there was a legitimate father somewhere in the vicinity. But a boy! Ah, a boy could grow up to be anything he had a mind to be. But most importantly he could grow up to be a *fardeener*. The promise of an extra *fardeener* or money-earner in a family was a rosy hope especially for a young immigrant couple who had come to the Golden Land with a dowry that consisted of a straw satchel containing a feather bed, two pillows, one heavy Russian silver spoon, and some dried fish (a hedge against starvation).

Well, I grew up to earn lots of money in this man's world, more than most boys grow up to earn, and though my contact with it has mostly been a pat in mid-air as it passed me on its way to the U. S. Internal Revenue Office, the implications of making it have always been more important than what the money could buy. In the advertising business, even more than most, how much you make tells how well you've made it. And though there are times, especially before each new campaign, when I still have doubts about being a writer, there's one thing I know in my heart—I'm a *fardeener*, Momma.

But no money ever seemed larger or more important to me than what I earned one Saturday before Christmas when I was about eleven, selling women's coats in the basement of a Brooklyn department store.

Twelve hours of work got me three dollars and change. I remember I had a large pocketbook with me that day but this first-earned money was much too precious to mingle with the remnants of my school allowance. Instead I clenched the three dollars and change tightly in my hand and held it that way during the long train ride home. When I got there, I could hardly open my fist and the dollars were wet and the coins were green. I put the money down carefully on the kitchen table in front of my mother like a supplication to the gods.

"See, Mom," I said, "even a girl can be a *fardeener*."

But that was when I was eleven. Up to the age of eight, I dressed up in boy's clothes for my mother's approval at every opportunity—Halloween, Thanksgiving, kids' masquerade parties. The clothes belonged to the boy next door. At one period I may have worn his clothes as often as he did but I was an early developer and soon the signs of girlness were too round to obscure. And suddenly the clothes no longer fit.

I remember that boy next door. We lived on the fourth floor of a walk-up tenement in the Jewish section of Brooklyn. Every Saturday night at bath time he would sneak out of his own flat and peek into ours through the keyhole. Not so much to glimpse my sister and me as we ran naked between the kitchen and the bathroom but because when we took off our long-sleeved, long-legged suits of underwear that were all stretched from wear and black with dirt at the seat, elbows, and knees, my mother would hold them up by the shoulders and make them dance in the air as she sang gay Russian songs. All day Friday a live fish swam in the bathtub waiting to be chopped into gefüllte fish for the Friday night dinner. But on Saturday night the tub was ours and Saturday night the underwear danced.

My mother had great joy in her. She could invest the most ordinary happenings with gaiety and excitement. And there was always music in our house. And parties. My mother could cook up a party out of a bag of potatoes—an extra bag of potatoes that my father might have bought at a bargain price from a passing pushcart. Suddenly the house would be full of hot delicious smells and the kitchen bustling with neighbors eating hot potato knishes right off the pan.

Even the purchase of a herring was cause for celebration. This invariably came wrapped in a page of Jewish newspaper. Potatoes would be put on to boil in their jackets while the herring was charred on hot ashes in the big black coal stove that dominated a corner of the kitchen.

In the few minutes it took for the neighbors to assemble, my mother's apron somehow changed to a brightly embroidered peasant blouse, topped by string on string of brightly colored beads. She was a very pretty lady with a clear sweet soprano voice that seemed so right for the lively Russian songs she sang. My father's baritone carried the harmony. With a little urging, he might even get out his violin and scrape away at it but that was mostly for laughs. Working around the clock didn't leave him too much time for practicing a violin.

Soon the house would be ringing with zesty folk songs and as often as not someone would break into a Russian folk dance. How we kids loved those parties. We loved the jokes and the laughter, and the smells and the tastes and staying up long after our bedtime.

My father was always bringing home bargain surprises for my mother. When it wasn't food from a horse-drawn wagon, it might be a little painted plate or vase or a cut glass bowl from quick-sellout places with names like "Cheap Charlie" or "Bargain Benny." Mostly these pieces had little chips or cracks, which was why they were such bargains, but after my mother had dipped them in hot sudsy water she would polish them up with a towel and show us proudly how the cut glass pieces reflected colored lights on the ceiling, like diamonds. In America, getting close to diamonds was not an impossible dream.

The wonderful thing about those Russian Jewish immigrants who came to this country to avoid conscription into the Czar's army, where life for the Jewish soldiers was especially hazardous, was their fantastic optimism and their ability to make jokes in the face of what must have seemed like imminent financial disaster.

I remember one snowy morning my father took my sister and me on a sleigh ride. We had a game. He would run fast, pulling the sled up and down the curbs with a little jerk, until one or both of us fell off into the snow, and pretend he didn't know he had lost us. The fun was when he found us again. One time we fell off near a pushcart that was selling neckties. My sister could read a little by then so we knew that the sign said, "Neckties 39¢ each." About an hour later, when we came back, it was much colder. We saw that the peddler had altered his sign. It now read "39¢ Neckties 10¢. I don't care!"

My father, we thought, was the tallest man in the whole world. He was about five feet eight and never weighed more or less than a hundred and thirty-eight pounds. His hair was thick and wavy; a true blue-black that gradually turned pure white without thinning out. He had a dark complexion, large green eyes, and strong white teeth. A full set (all his own as he often pointed out) that he owed to two important facts: one, as a boy in Russia, he had cleaned his teeth with coal, and, two, his father had told him always to put his right shoe on first. This he continued to do for the rest of his life. When he died at eighty-four, most of his teeth were his own.

My father's father had owned a lumberyard in Russia, so naturally Poppa's first job in America was in a lumberyard. But here he started at the bottom and carried lumber on his back all day long, sometimes for more than fourteen hours. At night my mother would unbend his back and, since supper was served rather late, he would go into the parlor and lean against the brown leather lounge or "lunj," as they used to call it. He never admitted to dozing or napping. That would have been too much of an admission of indulgence. He just "leaned" against the couch while we kids tiptoed around pretending not to hear the light snoring.

My father had a great deal of education for a Jewish immigrant at the turn of the century. But then, as I said, his father had owned a lumberyard, which was pretty good for a small-town Jew in Czarist Russia. He was very learned in many subjects, with a particular bent for mathematics and a fine background in literature.

My mother had no formal education at all. She had taught herself to read and write in Russian and Yiddish. Orphaned at the age of six, she had been raised by some distant cousins who had allowed her to read their schoolbooks when she wasn't earning her keep doing chores on their farm. It was a farm in the Ukraine, which she always described as wheat-colored. And she was wheat-colored too. Fair and blonde with fine strong cheekbones, golden-yellow eyes, and a warm, mother-y smell.

Her great desire was to become as American as possible, as soon as possible. She was one of the first ladies in her tenement to smoke a cigarette, to cook "American style," which merely meant undercooking instead of overcooking, to use green vegetables instead of just meat and potatoes, to send the "wash" out to the laundry instead of boiling it over the stove, and to get her home-baked bread at the German bakery store. But she never lost her touch with the pastries or the soft twisted white breads and special little cakes and cookies and knishes that made Friday nights and Jewish holidays so delicious.

And because being called a "regular Yankee" was her idea of the highest compliment anyone could receive, she sought out and enrolled in the neighborhood school that stayed open at night to teach the young foreigners to read, write, and spell in English. It didn't take long for her to learn how to read. I remember the soft cadences of her accent as she used to read us to sleep with a story from Grimm's *Fairy Tales*. It wasn't until I grew up that I realized how nicely, how precisely she used her English vocabulary. But the spelling continued to defeat her.

All through the years, when my sister and I did our homework, my mother practiced her spelling with a pencil on a white ruled pad. But it seems that in Russian and Yiddish one writes phonetically. And no matter how hard and how long she worked on her spelling, for the rest of her life she continued to write words the way she pronounced them—with a Yiddish accent.

Munday

Dear Shirley:

I am enjoying my wisit with Lillian. She and Hermann look vunderful. I came off the trane with a pane in my beck. Lillian is such a vorryer, she simplee insisstid we should go rite away to the doktor. First thing he esks me is how old am I. So I tole him fourtee. So Lillian sez pleas moma, I am fourtee. So all rite I am making a joak.

He screwtenized me all ova and tells me for my age I am okay. This I new myself. I esk Lillian where did she meet this big thinker. At the temple. So maybe he is a pieyus man, beddah with the bibel then with the medikal books becuss the pane in my beck, I still hav.

Lillian is vorking very hard with the orfans. Seems they are underfed from under food. So tell popa to itt. You must remind him becuss he forgets.

My lov to you and popa and the cat. Just see she shouldn't swing from the new kurtains.

I mis you.

Yours truly,
momma

My sister Lillian was only thirteen months old when I was born. What my parents didn't need at that time was another mouth to feed or another baby to crowd into their three-room flat. Even in those days it was possible to find an abortionist, usually a doctor who had escaped from another country and, denied a license in America, was restricted to an underground practice. But I was an accident that was allowed to happen on the chance that I might turn out to be a boy. All the neighbors predicted it from the way my mother carried me during her pregnancy. Nothing in the back. Everything up front. Come to think of it, that's the way I carried my own two girls, so maybe the odds then as now were fifty-fifty.

Anyway, my parents were ready with the name Leo. As it was, they called me Sherryl after my grandmother, which they translated into Sadie, Sarah, and finally Shirley as the most American equivalent. However, they raised me as a Leo. I was the "boy" in a family of three girls. Worse still, I was a Jewish "boy" growing up in an Irish neighborhood. My mother, like any other self-respecting Jewish mother, was mobilized upward.

The next step upward from the Jewish ghetto of Brownsville in Brooklyn was the Irish neighborhood on the outskirts of what is now the Williamsburg section of Brooklyn. Today, Brownsville is black and Williamsburg is the stronghold of Hassidic Jews, a deeply Orthodox sect who are holding their ground against the expanding Puerto Ricans, much as the Irish had resisted the Jews.

So we moved onward and upward from the Jewish ghetto into the Irish ghetto where they weren't particularly happy to welcome us. We were not only fair game as new kids, we were Jew kids. I used to walk around with my hands jammed into the pockets of my mackinaw trying to sound like a tough guy, "Okay, okay. Who pushed my sister?" I was scared stiff some kid would answer. But we were only girls, so they'd push us some more and run away.

Halloween night was a special open season for Jews. Pity the poor old man who still wore a beard and ventured into that neighborhood. He could be beaten up mercilessly. A rock in a swinging sock was the favorite weapon, a non-technological forerunner of the Saturday night special.

We were coming home at sundown this particular Halloween —my father, mother, and their two little girls. Suddenly the stones started flying. My mother, for the moment carried back to the old country she had escaped from, screamed "It's a pogrom! A pogrom!" My father gathered us to him and tried to shield us with his body. As the gang closed in on us, one kid recognized my father, who had that morning helped him fix his skate wagon, a wooden grocery box attached to a plank fitted with half a skate in front and half in back. "Hey, fellers, wait!" he shouted to his friends. "That's old man Polykoff. He's a good Jew." The rocks stopped. The gang escorted us home. My father was very proud. We had made it with the Irish.

But this still wasn't the America of my mother's dreams. One day, from the open platform of a wooden elevated train, she saw it. Flatbush. Open spaces. Green trees. A place to breathe. If my sister and I hadn't had the whooping cough, she might have missed it. The whooping cough was what got us permission to ride on the platform of the wooden train bound for Coney Island's salubrious salt air.

My father futilely protested the miles of cemeteries and grave-stones, the unpaved streets. He believed along with Thomas Wolfe that "only the dead know Brooklyn." But some very alive kids knew Brooklyn too. I have some wonderful memories of that long-ago Flatbush. Of open lots that froze over for ice skating. Some days we could even skate all the way to school. Of long stretches of snowy fields with hills for belly-whopping and snow fights, wearing a heavy wool sweater with scarf and hat to match, crocheted by my mother. Bright orange for my sister Lillian. Bright red for me. Of wonderful June mornings when we woke up at dawn, got into bathing suits, and drove in my father's Model T Ford to Coney Island for a quick dip in the ocean before school. Of living across the street from Mrs. Van Roedich's Nursery with rows and rows of wild-colored flowers that changed with the seasons. Of picnics in Prospect Park with the kids from the Junior Pleasure Club, a sobriquet we earnestly gave ourselves to indicate our age and our inclinations even though there was no Senior Pleasure Club that we knew of.

Of playing baseball in the gutter when the boys let us because baseball was such an American game. Of coming home alone from my first high school football game and cheering all the way home at the top of my lungs so that people flung open their windows to see what kind of parade was causing so much commo-tion, only to find that it was just one girl leaping along and yelling, "Team! Team! Team!"

Of my friendship in high school with a girl who lived on Seventh Street and Avenue J while I lived on Ninth Street and Avenue P. On the coldest winter nights when we were wound up talking about our dreams, I walked her home, then she would walk me home, and then we'd turn around and I'd walk her home again, unafraid in the dark, with our coats wide open, daring the wind to blow its fiercest. "Young America challenging the ele-ments," that's how we thought of ourselves. Sometimes when I got undressed my skin would be wind-chafed and red from neck to knees. But we were invincible, indomitable. The future was ours, provided we worked hard in school, brought home good marks, and listened to our parents. Quite independently, after a painful inventory, we decided we'd better develop our personalities too, since it didn't look as though we were going to be pretty enough to make it on looks alone.

So we tried to learn everything we could from "How to . . ." books. "How to Be a Fascinating Woman" in ten little pamphlets. "How to Make a Hit with Influential People" in one big book. "How to Be a Success at a Party" by making small talk. "How to Learn the Piano" in twelve easy lessons so no one would laugh when you sat down to play. The piano lessons didn't quite work. So my father had to scrape up the money to give us individual lessons. But that was all right because, in most Jewish families at that time, "advantages to the children" was a first consideration.

Nor was talent necessarily a contributing factor. Invariably the girls learned piano and the boys violin. I remember a vague sense that this must have something to do with the anatomy of the sexes. Didn't the boys stand up and the girls sit down for other functions?

We were taught to have great respect for literature. The public library was more important in our house than the synagogue. We went to Sunday School once a week so that we could learn to be proud to be Jewish. We went to the synagogue on Yom Kippur and Rosh Hashanah because we were afraid not to. But we went to the public library almost every day on our way home from school. Besides, it was the only acceptable excuse for coming home late.

We did our homework first and fast! Then we practiced the piano. Thirty minutes with the clock ticking alongside. Finally, finally, we'd get to our books. Time was longer when there was no T.V.

But the books, fascinating as they were, taught us the excitement of the past. School seemed only to prepare one for more schooling and that was okay. There were no arguments against school.

Every Jewish kid knew that schooling was the open-sesame to the future and free schooling was one of the big advantages of growing up in the New World. I could almost feel the vibrations in the classroom when the history teacher, quoting from President

James Monroe, told us, "The past belongs to the Old World but the future belongs to America."

But on a more immediate level it was from the magazine advertisements that we really learned how to be truly American.

How a home should look. How a table should be set. How to dress. How to be well groomed. Not only from the "How to . . ." books that we could get free by just mailing in a coupon with X number of coins to cover the cost of handling, but from the ads themselves. From the ads we learned how to rearrange the furniture, how to look nonchalant by smoking a cigarette, how to appear soigné by not ordering chicken salad every time you went out on a date.

Advertising. It was an American phenomenon. It taught the immigrants that they could achieve a clean complexion by using the soap used by nine out of ten screen stars. It alerted them to the possibility of offending without knowing it. For "within the curve of a woman's arm," even the daintiest woman's arm, toilet water would not be enough. It told them what their best friends might never tell them so they could take precautions to avoid the shame of being "often a bridesmaid but never a bride."

There was one ad we felt very close to. "Will they holler 'Skinny' when they see you at the beach?" My sister Lillian was very thin as a child. My mother was always cooking special foods and making beef teas to build her up. Not only as a matter of health but because in those days to be skinny meant you didn't have enough to eat, that you weren't quite making it in America. That was very important to the immigrants who had fled from poverty and severely circumscribed diets. I remember when my father tried to matchmake a young nephew to a buxom Russian girl. "She's a *graysa*, a *grubba*," he said, glorifying her ample proportions. She would not only be outward evidence of his financial success but mating with her would be like falling into a feather bed.

Advertising. It was a window into the life of America. Through it, you could look right into the homes of real people. See how they look. See how they act. Learn to do as they did.

But who were these people anyway? Where did they get them? Who wrote down what they said? Who made the pictures? How did they get into the *Saturday Evening Post, Liberty* magazine, the *Woman's Home Companion?*

One day when I was about twelve I read a Campbell's soup ad inviting readers to send in little verses about the delicious flavor of its tomato soup. They were using four-line rhymes illustrated with what looked like little Kewpie dolls, and they were called the Campbell kids. My entry suggested an illustration of three Kewpie dolls dressed as sailors marching with three Kewpie dolls dressed as soldiers. The four-line verse read:

> We're hearty men so brave and bold
> We eat a hearty meal.
> So give to us the rich red soup
> That bears the Campbell seal.

The response to the entry was good. It came with a congratulatory letter from Campbell's and a few cans of soup. But there was another letterhead included that intrigued me. On it was the name of an advertising company. That meant that there were actually companies with real people who knew all these things about how to live and dress and act and capture an ideal. I studied the names carefully. Ward Wheelock. They were so unforeign.

Could any girl, even one brought up to think like a Jewish "son," ever make it in such a gentile business? I remembered a remark overheard on the subway: "Yeah, but we have one Jewish gal around to keep the books straight. And Carter's secretary, I think she's one too, types a beautiful letter." Well, I hated arithmetic, so the bookkeeping was out. But maybe, just maybe, I could make it as a secretary.

2

Every Woman Should
Be Fired at Least Once

In the twenties Dorothy Parker wrote, "Men seldom make passes at girls who wear glasses." And Ogden Nash wrote, "Candy is dandy but liquor is quicker." And since Nash was then an advertising writer and I had written "The light in her vestibule is very detestibule . . ." maybe the time was right for me to venture into the craft.

But not everyone agreed.

I was a teen-age secretary at *Harper's Bazaar*. One day the big opportunity came. It was a pre-holiday weekend. The place had cleared out hours ago. Came a call from *Cosmopolitan* magazine. *Harper's Bazaar* was scheduled to run an ad in their October issue. Where was it? They needed copy right away. Could I do it?

No problem. I stepped into the breach and did it!

The ad told all about the famous authors who were scheduled to appear in the next month's *Bazaar* and the only thing I did wrong was to misspell the names of a few authors. I remember the featured author was Robert Hichens. Robert Hechins? Robert Hochens? Or was it Robert Huchens?

After I was fired I went to the country and cried for a week. The extra weight in my pay envelope had not been a big raise as I had hoped but a large rejection slip. Instead of seeing the ad as splendid evidence of initiative and responsibility, the publisher had stormed into the editor's office. He was wearing a pale green fedora. He whipped it off, threw it on the floor, and stomped on it. It was his favorite hat.

The editor blamed the staff copywriter, who blamed my boss, the circulation manager, who said he didn't blame me at all though he did deplore the loss of a good secretary.

It was then that I vowed I would get even with *Harper's Bazaar*. Spelling or no spelling, I'd make it as an ad writer. So you see, everyone should be fired at least once in her life.

It's only as I write this now that I wonder whether my bad spelling was just another evidence of my identification with my mother. How often she used to say—and this was way before women's lib—"If I were only born in America, I would have made a career for myself." Well, I was born in America. And a funny thing happened on the way to my career.

Harper's Bazaar sold a lot of subscriptions from that ad I wrote for *Cosmopolitan*. Not that it was so different from the ones that had already run. And this is the point of the story. People are inherently kind. Or so I've always believed. They probably caught the misspelling and thought, "Ohhhh, someone's going to catch it for this," and sent in the coupons for subscriptions.

However, it took several months to find this out. And by that time it was too late for *Harper's Bazaar*. I had already been hired as a copywriter by a women's fashion and specialty store in Brooklyn for a curious reason. I was a blonde. And that store was run by four bachelor brothers who were mad for blondes. In my innocence, I thought it was the sample ads I had prepared but it seems that I mostly intrigued them as a sex object. I don't remember minding that though I did have the reputation of being the last virgin in Brooklyn.

The hidden trap here was that, if you were silly enough to date any one of them, one of the others would get you fired. A kind of Russian roulette, Brooklyn style. It was all very titillating for a teen-ager.

I learned a lot of things there.

I learned that in order to get a job you had to be a bargain. But if you were female you had to be a crazy bargain. I had been making $45 a week at *Harper's Bazaar*. This was before the minimum wage laws and I was happy to take $19 a week just to break into the field I had dreamed of. In those days, blondes were supposed to be beautiful but dumb. I was neither. But I did have some sexy measurements. By the end of the year I had been raised to $85 a week. And two years later I was chosen "Miss Fulton Street" in an interstore contest. Or maybe I was just a runner-up "Miss Fulton Street" but it accounted for the fact that the next to the youngest brother suddenly became very interested in the advertising department. He had a dimple, a cleft chin, and an Arrow-collar profile as done by James Montgomery Flagg. Or Norman Rockwell, if you're younger.

Those were days of affluence. It was 1929 before the great Wall Street crash. The "kept" woman was an institution. And the "sugar daddy" was willing to pay. The lavishly furred cloth coats that came up for ads were priced around $800 or $900. That's pretty much what they are today but the economy was far, far different then. An $800 or $900 cloth coat was practically better than a mink.

This next-to-youngest brother would bring these coats up personally and toss one at me. "Here, you! Try this one on."

I sure was one lousy model. Not a bit soigné. But then, I had been brought up to use my brain, not my body. I remember one particular coat, a rich tweed lavish with fox trim. He buttoned the fur under my chin and whispered, "Why don't you borrow this next time you have an important date?" I didn't have dates that could accommodate anything that affluent but the suggestion sparked the headline: "Look like you're going to the races when you're only racing to the grocer's."

One time I was wearing a rhinestone necklace, a string of beauty especially selected from a Woolworth counter. It fell to the floor. He picked it up and clasped it around my neck. "These could be real diamonds," he whispered against my cheek.

I learn fast. The next week my ad, "Rhinestones, a girl's next best friend," was a complete sellout for a jewelry promotion.

One evening I worked late. I was so tired, I just grabbed my coat and left the office. My face was smudged, my hair hung down in limp strands. I was hardly at my best. As I shlumped through the darkened store to the side exit, I met him looking immaculate in dinner clothes.

"What are you doing here?" he asked.

"Working," I said.

"Come, I'll take you home."

"I have to call my mother."

"There's a phone booth in back."

He led me through the dark at the head of the stairs. I dialed the number. He joined me in the booth. He kissed me.

"Why are you trembling?" he asked.

My mother kept saying, "Hello, hello."

Still trembling, I walked out with him to the street.

"That's my car," he said, pointing to a big black Pierce-Arrow limousine. And as I hesitated he said, "Come on. Get in."

Bravely, I got in. To get to my home, a small unimpressive two-family house, we had to drive through what was then called the "Blue Book" section of Brooklyn because that was where the Social Registerites lived. As we went by a huge Southern-type mansion on what must have been a double-acre lawn, I thought, "Oh, if I could only say I lived here." As if in response, the car stopped. For a moment, my heart did too. God had heard me. But that's where he lived. "I'll be out in a minute," he said. When we finally got to my block, there was my father pacing up and down in front of the house. After all, I was only eighteen and it was ten o'clock.

"It's ten o'clock," my father said sternly to this thirty-year-old man. "What are you doing out so late?"

My father had many ways of discouraging our suitors. When my sister or I were out on a date, promptly at ten he would put out all the lights except for the very bright one in the hall which was what made our "vestibule so detestibule." In addition, he would leave the shirt he had just taken off in the middle of the living-room sofa. This was to indicate that he was at home and nearby and that it was late enough for any self-respecting person to be in bed.

To circumvent this, my sister and I perfected a technique. With one swift sweep of the hand, we'd gather up the shirt, toss it behind the sofa, and pull the cord that lit up the living-room lamp.

What did I learn on that first job in advertising? I learned that romance in an office is a most unequal contest. So I guess you can never call me that *Cosmopolitan* girl.

As time went on, I learned that humor can be a most effective tool but only if the consumer is on the right side of the joke. Those were happy days before the Great Depression. When one department store ran an ad for floral print nightgowns with the headline, "When nighties are in flower," my nightgown sale read, "A thousand and one nighties." Another store ran petticoats with "Slips that pass in the light." I countered with "A sale to launch a thousand slips." Everyone had fun and everyone prospered.

At another time, when the Dies Committee was looking all over and under the bed for Communist activators, even threatening to investigate little Shirley Temple, I started a great new fashion color, "Non-subversive Red!"

But as time went on and the economy grew harder I learned that, when a client is prepared to spend millions of dollars on a single product, humor may not be enough—that is, if the consumer is to be moved to buy instead of to laugh.

In the early 1940s, while working at my second advertising agency, a small company whose client roster consisted mainly of women's shoes, I also learned how to juggle half a dozen campaigns simultaneously for the same type of product. Maybe that's why I'm always so mystified by that big agency trauma: conflicts. In a big agency, if a client makes a toothpaste, the agency may not accept another client who also makes a toothpaste even though the agency has not been assigned a toothpaste by either company. In these happy days of acquisitions and mergers, this makes getting new business more than a bit of a problem for an agency.

At Frederick-Clinton in the forties, however, we didn't worry about such things. At the same time that I was writing retail ads for the Kitty Kelly Shoe Chain, $3.95, I was writing ads for Vogues by Jamsie, $7.50, a somebody-or-other from St. Louis, $9.50 retail, Mademoiselle Shoes by Carlisle (an I. Miller subsidiary), $13 to $20, and Andrew Geller Shoes, $25 and up and up.

The only time it was even the slightest strain was the three weeks before Easter when every client was scheduled to run two ads on navy blue and one ad on patent leather. That's twelve for navy and six for patent, all scheduled to run more or less in the same newspapers and magazines at the same time.

In self-defense, I created a separate personality in my mind for each account. And just as a mother of six feels drawn to each child for its own particular qualities, I valued each account for its own distinct characteristics. And like a mother, every time I did a little something special for one child, I felt it incumbent to do a little something special for the others. The results were much better ads than I might have produced were I not competing with myself all of the time. (This training stood me in good stead later on during my tenure at Foote, Cone & Belding, where I worked simultaneously on three major haircoloring products and four or five smaller ones for their client, the Clairol Company. I just used one of my heads for each product.)

The shoe business was fun. "Build up your ego, amigo," was the campaign I did for Adler Elevated Shoes to appeal to the newly arriving Puerto Rican men who were finding American women a bit tall. I was also in at what was practically the beginning of advertising for the Mademoiselle Shoe Company. (Where are they now?) Their appeal, as the name would indicate, was to the young high school, college, and career types. I was pretty young myself then so it was easy to enter into the spirit with "Mademoiselle—you'll love to be in our shoes!" and to work with the bright young people in the design shop on the first ballet shoe for street wear that was to prove a fantastic seller for years. "Balletina.: turns walking into a dancing thing."

With Andrew Geller, we did other innovative things. Like the introduction of the opera pump. "Andrew Geller, the Place de l'Opera. On the left bank of 57th Street." And because the forties were an era of elegance and great femininity in clothes (Dior's dazzling New Look with the dipping hemline, all curvy in the waist, the return of Chanel with all her easy elegance, the Clare McCardells—so fresh, so admiring of the American woman's body), the toe of our classic, ladylike opera got pointier and pointier, the heel higher and thinner until it became what we called the "Diminuen-toe with the Stiletto heel." These terms later became generic. However, today when I look down at my twisted feet barely wedged into wide, wide toes and low, low heels for the twenty-six-block walk to my office, I'm prepared to admit that we may have overdone it with the stilettos. But they were a lot more flattering than the seventies' Minnie Mouse feet, which are probably no less destructive. Some things in the seventies haven't changed at all: seems they are still playing my song from the fifties, "Chock Full O'Nuts is that heavenly coffee. . . ."

When I think of the shoe business I always remember with affection Mr. J. P. Levy of Boston. He manufactured and retailed four or five different retail shoe chains. All with different names, all competitive with each other, and all located in stores on the same big shopping street in big cities.

Having had all this experience in shoes, I was now typecast as a shoe expert. Mr. Levy had heard I had retired after my second child was born, to write short stories at home, and he wondered if I could spare two or three days a week to do freelance advertising for his various chains.

I was doing rather well with the short stories. I sold three out of five. The one I remember most, because it irrevocably changed my life, went for a whopping $48. Not bad when you consider it took me only four months to write it. It was about a career woman who stops working to stay home and raise a baby, but realizes, after a year, that she is longing to resume her job. She hires a "nana" and in a tearful moment sees that the nurse has to some extent taken her place in the child's affections. In the denouement, she comes to accept this fact as part of the price she must pay to have a career—and decides she is willing to pay it. The irony is that the editors forced me to change the ending to make her realize that she *won't* pay that price, and the final line of the story was revised to read:

> Gwen went into the bathroom and wept deep, exhausting sobs . . . but when the storm subsided, she realized she had been weeping mostly for her job. . . . Suddenly she stopped and smiled. Better take off the negligee. It might get spotted. It would be a good idea to make her clothes last as long as possible, now that she was about to become just plain Mrs. William B. Carstairs, housewife.

That actually was my exit line; like Nora in *A Doll's House*, after I delivered that sentence to the magazine's editors, I walked out the door. Never to be a housewife again. I telephoned Mr. Levy in Boston and told him I was intrigued with his money and his viewpoint.

"You know, Shirley," he said during the interview, "you're looking at a Communist [pronounced Commonist]. I'm giving the masses the best God-damned shoe in America for only $3.95."

"At a slight profit?" I asked.

"Let's not quibble," he answered.

As I became more experienced with agency-client relations, I learned how to interpret and swing to the special idiom of the clients. I even had my own little Samuel Goldwyn who said in response to a terrific job offer that someone had received, "I know. The grass is always greener where the grass is greener," or in his criticism of a campaign just completed, "Maybe that's a little too ritzy. Why don't you try something a little more guttural?" But my favorite was the corset-bra manufacturer who said, "I want something elegant, really high class. Something that'll bite them in the ass." So I suggested he uplift his 38D figures with the line "Her cup runneth over." "*That's* class," he said; it took an hour to unsell him.

The drawback of being typecast as a certain kind of copywriter did not come home to me until just before I went to Foote, Cone & Belding, when I was called up to bring my sample book to a now defunct agency that had the Clairol haircoloring account. The copy chief approved of my particular style of writing. "They're great ads," he said, "but you have no haircoloring experience."

But some people just can't escape their fate. Two months later I began working at Foote, Cone & Belding. I'd only been there a few days when the F. C. & B. copy chief came by, tossed some papers on my desk, and said, "Guess what, Polykoff, we just got the Clairol Company. It's yours, honey, on account you're the only one around here who can write that kind of schmaltz."

3

Does She . . .
Or Doesn't She?

I guess my whole life wrote that campaign.

There are advertising campaigns that seem terribly smart, bright, slick, humorous, written to impress the copywriting colleague down the hall, or even to show off one's own wit to oneself, but I have always believed that ads that communicate, ads that really create a compelling person-to-person bond, are ads that reflect the writer's total life experience. I know that sounds a little big, even pompous, but if an ad writer is willing to expose her honest reactions not only to the product but, more importantly, to the significance of the product in terms of the emotional needs it fulfills (as well as its practical utility), she will be able to distill those aspects of the product that are its genuine selling points.

Since I like to think of this as a book on advertising, let's examine the premise that my whole life wrote it, that everything that has contributed to me as a person also has contributed to the campaigns I create.

Being an awkward seven-year-old middle child between two beautiful brunette sisters was a fundamental factor in this first Clairol campaign. The older one, Lillian, was lovely enough to have been photographed nude on a white fur rug. The youngest, Ellenore, was so pretty people were always stopping the carriage to admire her. As far as I knew, nobody ever photographed me nude on a white fur rug or stopped the carriage to admire me. But I had blonde hair like my mother's, though most of her friends assured me I'd never be as pretty.

So the way I felt at fifteen, when my hair began to darken and I began periodic visits to Mr. Nicholas—beauty parlor one flight up—wrote that campaign too. Little gray-haired Mr. Nicholas and I maintained a pleasant fiction. He didn't bleach my hair. He just lightened the back a little to match the front. And the back kept getting closer to the front. But nobody seemed the wiser, and whatever compliments I got continued to be about my "naturally" blonde hair, which was just like my mother's, to whom a beauty parlor was the room you fixed up and used only for company.

Or maybe it was something that happened to me in 1933. I had just met George. I had known him three weeks when he invited me to Passover dinner in Reading, Pee-ay. In 1933, if you lived in New York and a fellow invited you to come meet his family in Reading, Pee-ay, it was tantamount to a proposal of marriage. I had been dragging along with two other fellows for about five years, neither of whom had ever asked me to come home and meet the family. So I was very excited about the idea and I accepted.

George's father was an Orthodox rabbi. He was tall and handsome with a beard which seemed to get smaller through the years as he grew to feel more American. And he liked to tell jokes. He and I hit it off right away. George's mother, on the other hand, was a rather silent, old-fashioned lady who wore a severe, pulled-back, tight haircomb, one step away from the *sheitel*, a wig worn by Orthodox women to cover the shaven head since hair was an unseemly adornment for a respectable Orthodox matron. It was quite obvious that she adored her son. It was also quite obvious that the whole family adored him. He was the second child and the oldest boy, the first to break away from the family and go to live in the big city, where he had studied law and graduated at the head of his class. The girl he brought home would have to be very special. I remember vividly how much I wanted to be very special for just this one time.

The Passover dinner was traditional. Very lavish and heavy. As a charter member of the clean plate club, I ate everything that was put before me. Soup, stuffed derma, overroasted chicken, a sweet potato and prune dish called tsimmes, sponge cake, tea with lemon, and a mixed fruit gelatine. After all, who has to tell a middle child how to get on the right side of any mother?

But I could hardly wait to start the drive home to find out how I had done.

"How'd I do, George?" I said as soon as the car started. "Did your mother like me?"

"The twins adored you."

"But what did *she* say?"

"My sister Mildred thought you were great. So sophisticated."

"That's nice, George. But what did *she* say?"

Pause. Like in a Pinter play.

"She says you paint your hair." Pause again. "Well, do you?"

I managed to say, "I do," but that was three weeks later before a justice of the peace.

That day I merely scrunched down on my side of the car. But I could hear his mother thinking as she cleared away the dishes:

"*Zee paint dos huer? Odder zee paint dos nicht? Zee paint dos huer? Odder zee paint dos nicht?*" Freely translated, that means "Does she . . . or doesn't she?"

So maybe my mother-in-law wrote the line.

Twenty years later, in 1955, Clairol, the haircoloring company, came to Foote, Cone & Belding, the advertising company, and thus began one of the most compatible relationships in the annals of client and agency.

In that twenty-year interim between *Harper's Bazaar* and Foote, Cone, my life had moved along two clearly defined paths—one headed toward marriage (there was no other legitimate goal for a girl in my generation) and the other toward realizing myself in a job, as a man might, had I been born the boy my mother wanted.

In the career department, I had risen from my beginning job in the Brooklyn store to the top fashion-writing job in Bamberger's and then Kresge's Department Store. Both were located in Newark, New Jersey. The trip from Brooklyn to Newark and back, by way of two wildly overcrowded subways and one foul-smelling shuttle over the Jersey meadows, took better than three hours a day.

I hated that trip. I hated the angry pushing in the subways, having to clutch my pocketbook or hat to keep it from being pulled away as the crowds surged in and out at each station. (Once they managed to rip off the tail of my beautiful new cross fox scarf that I had saved for for so long.) I hated having to hold my body in and away from some stranger's unfulfilled sex urge. Even getting a seat was no protection. Sooner or later some guy hanging onto the overhead strap, his head safely hidden behind his newspaper, would sway back and forth until somehow he managed to wedge his leg between your knees so he could ride up your thighs when the train lurched.

I hated the trip back in the evening at the end of a long hard day but I was ashamed to be a quitter so I used to wish for a small accident like a light tap by a light automobile as I was crossing the street. Or that I might have to undergo a small surgical operation like having my appendix removed, so I could resign from the job without losing face with myself.

But I admired the people I worked with in Newark. They were hard merchants, bright and aggressive, and I learned a lot from them, not only about writing but in merchandising and marketing, which were of inestimable value to me in the three advertising agencies I worked for later and in my own agency now. Retailing is a great school and some of those merchandise managers and promotion directors were top men in this very competitive field.

Together we must have produced some pretty good ads because they were always being picked up and reproduced on the covers of retail advertising publications as fine examples of fashion-co-ordinated or store-wide promotions. Because they were my writing and responsibility, it wasn't long before I received an offer I couldn't refuse from a New York advertising agency that needed someone with retail experience to handle the I. J. Fox account. I. J. Fox was a retail furrier who had recently moved from Sixth to Fifth Avenue and was prepared to blitz the city with an ad budget of about a million dollars, which was a lot of retail budget for one product in the middle thirties.

My personal life had also progressed. In 1933, around the bank holiday, I had acquired a husband. In the midst of the Depression, I had borne two daughters. And in the next ten years I had experienced all the problems of trying to hold onto a career so that the family wouldn't notice that I had one (although my daughters have since assured me that they certainly did notice) and to handle the home so that it wouldn't appear to the career that there even *was* a family that might make any claims on my attention.

There were a few times in the early part of my marriage, before the girls were born, and once after, when I did stop working because even in the depressed thirties it was not seemly to my husband's law partners for a wife to work.

But I didn't know how to act as a lady in retirement.

First, I became the perfect little helpmeet, primed each evening for George's return from his stint of work, happy to wait on him with newspaper and cooling wine and to ask interesting questions about his day at the office. He hated it.

"What the hell is going on here with you, anyway?" he yelled on about the third day. I must have looked so startled that he laughed and pulled me on his lap.

"Look, my friend, let's face it," he said. "The servile thing is not your style. It's just not your style!"

So I took to dashing about in our Plymouth roadster with the top down, wearing a large white linen hat and crisscross sandals, white cotton gloves, and suits to match the blue of the car. All very chic and with it, to meet the girls for lunch or a midafternoon cocktail. We were young and gay, as they used to say, and I could see right off, from the glances we got from men who seemed to have nothing better to do than hang around fancy bars, how a girl could get into a lot of trouble. So I knew that was not for me.

We had a maid whose name was Betty. She got six dollars and sixty cents carfare for six afternoons a week from two until after dinner. She was very black and skinny with gnarled hands and feet. And I loved the way she knew how to cook all the things George liked to eat and kept the apartment spotless. But I loved her the most one day when she came up from the laundry carrying a big basket of washed clothes. She was laughing and shaking her head.

"You know the girls downstairs didn't believe me when I told them I used to be a toe and tap dancer for ——" and she named a well-known band leader. "So I took off my shoes and these tired old feet got right up on their toes on that hard cee-ment floor and did a few turns. I showed 'em."

"You what?" I said, aghast.

She continued to laugh as she put down the basket, took off her shoes, and proceeded to show me too. And right before my eyes she turned from a plain, gnarled little old lady into a glowing, graceful little old sprite.

She used to wear a very thin, worn-out old coat even in the coldest weather so I gave her my raccoon coat. But the next day she was wearing the same thin, tired old coat.

"It's freezing," I said. "Why aren't you wearing the fur?"

"It's so pretty. I'm afraid you'll take it back."

"That's silly!" I said. "I gave it to you so you wouldn't get pneumonia." I kissed my pinky to the sky. "Look, I swear to God that I'll never take it back."

But I guess I didn't convince her because in about two weeks she left my job. So she could feel safer wearing the coat, I suppose.

Since I was still in retirement, I decided to have a whirl at the housework myself. But you couldn't live in a house I had cleaned. After I scrubbed the kitchen floor, I'd put newspapers down. If anyone smoked, I followed them around to make sure that only one ashtray was used. No more free and easy flicking from tray to tray when I had to wash them. And it must have been very trying to eat what I cooked because I watched every mouthful to see if the verdict was delicious.

George was very patient for about two weeks. Then one evening he came home with flowers.

"Listen, sweetie. You make a lousy little woman in the kitchen." He shook his head. "I find the whole performance very unconvincing. You know, I don't think you even know how to read a recipe. To double one of the ingredients doesn't necessarily improve the dish. Like the brandy you used in that stewed beef thing you made the other night."

And then, because he was master of the understatement, he added, "You know, I was drunk from that stew! It's the first time in my life that I was ever drunk from a stew!"

He paced the floor. "Poor George," he muttered. He always

spoke of himself in the third person when he felt he was being sorely tried. "Stewed on a stew!"

As for me, I felt trapped. I loved George, but I felt trapped. I didn't know what to do with myself. I didn't know how to act. I didn't know how to ask for money or how to account for it once it was spent. I felt guilty drawing checks on a joint account that I didn't contribute to but I hated even more to find money on the table on those mornings when George left before I awoke.

On the other hand, he didn't understand why having me draw a check was not preferable to taking his last twenty-dollar bill, leaving him with about one dollar in change or just enough for a taxi to the office if he walked the first six blocks.

Fortunately, George was a very bright guy with short tolerance for waste, a healthy respect for ability regardless of its sex, and great admiration for the few women he had encountered in business.

He couldn't stand me as a lady of leisure. Besides, he thought he had married a woman with definite opinions and independent interests. Instead, he found himself with a frightened and un-focused gadfly whose energy ranneth over—in all directions.

"I'm just one poor little man, not a whole stag line," he'd say with that mock sad expression we used to call his Jesus face (pronounced Hay-su Face-u). He was almost as happy as I when Mr. I. J. Fox phoned me direct and told me to stop fooling around and report to his agency by the following Monday.

And that's how I got back into the advertising business and even-tually to Foote, Cone & Belding.

In 1955 there was no haircoloring industry as we know it today. Haircoloring had about the same social acceptance as cigarettes and lipsticks had before the First World War. Only about seven per cent of the women in the country used haircoloring of any kind. Who were these women? They were models, actresses in the tradition begun by Jean Harlow, members of the jet set then called café society, a few brave career girls like me, and a select group known as "fast women."

In those days, if you found a gray hair, you pulled it out. So you can see that if you were really committed to no gray hair you could end up looking like Mahatma Gandhi. Recognizing the ambiguous status of haircoloring as a beauty product, it seemed very clear that our most important job would be to change the image of those who used haircoloring and to make the idea respectable. That would need a lot of thinking out.

I have a theory that one can only create bright thinking when one is feeling "up." If the mood is "down," forget it. Go take a brisk walk to get the circulation going. And sing "up" songs. I happen to react best to Dixieland. On days when the "down" mood is proof even against "Red Hot Momma" or "Louisville Lou," the ideas walk on flat feet. When the music takes hold, the ideas start skipping. I'm also a nut on beat. I like rhythm in copy, so I have to hear the words out loud. This has caused some people to look at me strangely. Some even cross the street. Obviously, getting the ideas for the first ads on haircoloring was going to take a lot of walking. And plenty of Dixieland.

Not only did we have to change the idea of the kind of woman who used haircoloring but we had a lot of other problems like fear of family disapproval. That could make a woman very anxious.

I remembered a traumatic happening when we were kids. The three of us left for school the same as usual but when we returned that afternoon what did we find? Momma with her hair bobbed! It shook our world. None of the other mothers we knew had bobbed hair. I remember that we cried. As for my father, he went into a state of shock that lasted for weeks. So what would happen to the average family unprepared for a momma who suddenly took it into her head to change the color of her hair?

And what about that other problem that I knew first hand? The fact that when a woman gets a compliment about her hair she wants very much to feel that she is being admired for a feature that is intrinsically her own, not something that comes out of a bottle. That is where haircoloring is different from most other cosmetics.

It became increasingly apparent to me that everything about the campaign would have to stress naturalness, a naturalness surrounded by an aura of great respectability.

So imbued did I become with the idea of removing the onus attached to haircoloring that it became almost a crusade with me to change even the words ordinarily associated with hair color. "To bleach" must become "to blonde" or "to lighten." As for the word "dye," it was to be eliminated, but completely, from the lexicon of haircoloring.

I remember one compliments-of-a-friend ad sent out to a souvenir journal of the Friars' Club which was honoring a well-known comedian. It read, "Laugh, I thought I'd tint (we never say 'dye')!"

But time was passing, deadlines were approaching. I had lots of feelings about it but I still had no campaign for Miss Clairol Hair Color until one night when George and I went to a party. George used to feel that when the law profession got him the advertising profession lost a brilliant copywriter, while I took the stance that I could solve all his complicated legal problems with just simple logic. He said that simple was the word for it, especially since my jurisprudence was usually arrived at "without fear or research." Because we liked each other's first reactions to ideas, we had gotten into the habit of trying things out on each other without warning. As though inadvertently.

At this particular party, a girl walked in with flaming red hair. He was drawn to red hair. I sidled over to him and whispered, "Does she . . . or doesn't she?"

"What?"

"You know. *Zee paint dos huer?*" His mother's query had become our favorite one-liner.

He gave me the "shark face." That's the lewd lopsided grin the shark wears in comic books when he senses the approach of a potential hemophiliac.

The next morning he said, "Hey, what are you doing about that hair-color job?"

"I told you last night. Does she . . . or doesn't she?"

He raised an eyebrow. "You wouldn't dare!"

"Why not?" I said. "Does she . . . or doesn't she? Or perhaps you prefer it in the original Yiddish?"

The raised eyebrow did it. The next morning I sent the following memo to the head art director. It was dated July 9, 1955.

On that stuff I talked to you about, Miss Clairol Hair Color Bath, I've got three approaches. One is great but I need at least two others for knock-downs at the meeting so I can sell the one I really want.

※1. *"Naturally by Miss Clairol."* We use the same model in each ad, a kind of fresh-faced creature, and each time her hair color is different but it always looks natural. (Yeah, I know. It's a nothing idea.)

※2. *"Tear up those baby pictures. I'm a redhead now!"* and then a pay-off line like: "No one will know you weren't born a redhead" (or blonde or whatever). It has a nice kind of exuberance combined with naturalness. Only I don't see these for long-term use and a good campaign has to snowball.

※3. Now here's the one I really want. If I can get it sold to the client. Listen to this: *"Does she . . . or doesn't she?"* (No, I'm not kidding. Didn't you ever hear of the arresting question?) Followed by: *"Only her mother knows for sure!"* or *"So natural, only her mother knows for sure!"*

I may not do the mother part, though as far as I'm concerned mother is the ultimate authority. However, if Clairol goes retail, they may have a problem of offending beauty salons, where they are presently doing all of their business. So I may change the word "mother" to "hairdresser." This could be awfully good business— turning the hairdresser into a color expert. Besides, it reinforces the claim of naturalness and, not so incidentally, glamorizes the salon.

The psychology is obvious. I know from myself. If anyone admires my hair, I'd rather die than admit I dye. And since I feel so strongly that the average woman is me, this great stress on naturalness is important.

So too for the models. No slick overly made-up fashion types. Our women must be like the gals in that book by Spectorsky, *The Exurbanites*. Shirtwaist types instead of glamor gowns. Cashmere-sweater-over-the-shoulder types. Like larger-than-life portraits of the proverbial girl on the block who's a little prettier than your wife and lives in a house slightly nicer than yours. Or the average model with her face washed. This, in itself, will be a new twist. All very P.T.A.-ish and ladylike, if you'll pardon the expression. Very avant garde, you must admit, to have a "lady" in a hair-coloring ad.

And let's put her in real-life situations. Like a mother with a child . . . maybe heads together doing homework . . . or out in the playground going down a slide . . . or sailing a boat with her kid in the park. I used to do that with my little girls until I was ready to drop. Anyway, kids are fun to have in an ad that asks, "Does she . . . or doesn't she?" wouldn't you say?

Think about this, Bill, but remember especially that everything about these ads has to come through as absolutely real, straightforward, and honest. Even the tiniest phony note will flaw what we're trying to accomplish.

For instance, the other night, it was about one in the morning, George and I stopped off at Ratner's on the East Side for some scrambled eggs and bagels. We were practically alone in the place and just about ready to call it a night when the door opened and in walked a beautiful young man, spotless in a navy-blue Bar Mitzvah suit, except that he was obviously Irish. He staggered over to a table near us and ordered some black coffee. He'd just escaped from being best man at his sister's wedding and was wondering aloud why his sister had wanted to marry the S.O.B. Suddenly he looked over at George.

"My name is O'Brien," he said, coming over to shake hands.

George, wanting to make him feel at home, said, "Hi. My name is Murphy."

O'Brien studied George's face a moment, then went back to his coffee with a puzzled look on his face. "Hey, Murph," he said after a while, "you're Jewish, aren't you?"

I'm not quite sure how this story applies, unless I'm just trying to say I don't want to fool some of the people even some of the time.

S.P.

Now here's how it was at that time in the middle fifties. On T.V., women were having love affairs with refrigerators and true-to-life raps with Procter & Gamble's Katy Winters. Bufferin (B's) were racing Aspirin (A's) from the stomach to the seat of the pain, while sinus cavities were being lit up and cleared out fast, fast, fast. The sell was hard, the voice-over was the voice of authority and the models mostly male because the research showed that, in the fifties, viewers were much too fine to watch a woman suffer. If you're watching in the seventies, however, you can see we've come a long way, baby.

On the other hand, magazine ads in the fifties, and I can't stress this enough, were almost entirely peopled with high-fashion, overly made-up, overly groomed "Park Avenue penthouse" types whose brilliant smiles reflected the sheer pleasure of mopping floors, baking cakes, and gentle laxative relief.

In contrast, I remembered my own first responses to those old *Saturday Evening Post* ads I had studied as a kid. To me, at that time, all those people had been real. That was their strength. And while I was more sophisticated now, I instinctively knew that if haircoloring ads were to have any acceptance at all the people portrayed as users would have to look like real live people. People you'd want to be like.

Not to mention the old advertising saw: "When everybody's zigging, zag."

So the art director sent out a call for fresh-faced models. In line with our discussions, he instructed them not to wear make-up and to bring their own clothes. First, to make sure we didn't exclude any woman from our appeal, we photographed models purporting to be schoolteachers, secretaries, etc. Then, following through on my memo, we added the child. For rapport and warmth and, yes, motherhood. But also to draw a comparison between the shiny quality of the Miss Clairoled hair to the soft, shining color of the child's hair.

All credit to the client. After the first mother and child ad appeared, schoolteacher and secretary alone already having run, they sent down a memo stipulating that we never drop the mother and child identification. This indeed turned out to be a most valuable contribution.

So busy were we establishing an aura of respectability that we almost overlooked a small but important point. The name of the product was *Miss* Clairol. In 1955, unwed motherhood was not yet chic. As I stood there literally wringing my hands under the photographer's bright lights, I caught the glint of my gold wedding band. The pictures were reshot, the campaign was saved, and the ring finger of the model's left hand became an important prop in every Miss Clairol illustration.

As I approach the body copy of the ads, it might be well for me to characterize my own particular style of copywriting. It's rarely about products to a consumer. It is more a direct conversation *with* the consumer about the product. Like a sales clerk. But friendly.

Miss Clairol was the first real campaign about hair color. In 1955, speaking directly to a woman about the color of her hair was much too impertinent. So these ads were one woman talking to another but in the oblique way that people tell you intimate details about themselves but say it happened to a friend. Instead of head-on confrontation, we started each ad as though we were discussing the girl in the photograph, a "nice" woman we both knew.

"Her looks are exciting, her manner is gentle and this is a lovely thing in a woman." "Are mothers getting younger, or do they just look that way?" "She's as much fun as a kid and just as fresh looking." I remember how I sweated over those first lines of body copy. Somewhere in the middle of the copy we would switch from the girl in the photograph to the reader's own hair and how much our product could do to improve her looks and outlook.

The whole tone of the ad was reassuring. Sympathetic, like a pat on the head. And very understanding. And smack in the middle of all this understanding and middle-class morality, we placed the arresting question, the bombshell—"Does she . . . or doesn't she?"

Then quickly to answer the question and bring the mind back from wherever it went, we followed with our second line, "Hair color so natural only her hairdresser knows for sure."

We still had the whole business of family resistance to overcome and here we almost lost out altogether. Until 1955, beauty products of any kind were advertised almost entirely in fashion books like *Vogue* or *Harper's Bazaar*. Or in strictly women's magazines like *McCall's, Ladies' Home Journal,* movie magazines, or *True Story.* What we needed was a family magazine like *Life.* The strategy of using *Life* magazine for haircoloring at that time was in itself very innovative and required courage on the part of the client. But courage pops up in unexpected places. This time the client was happy but *Life* was not. They turned us down. It took a lot of guts to turn down ten pages in full color in those days, especially when the ten pages could open up an entirely new category that the magazine had been panting for. But it seemed that *Life* suddenly had a rush of principles to the head. *Life,* whose comprehensive editorial un-coverage had sometimes taken such a dramatic form as bikini girls on the cover or center spread, turned the campaign down as too suggestive.

Foote, Cone & Belding itself was divided into two camps. One group, composed mostly of men, said, "Honey, you must be kidding. You'll never get away with that!"

This had a familiar ring. I had heard all that from George on the morning that I sent out the original memo. If I lost this battle, I'd have to live with his raised eyebrow for the rest of my life.

Fortunately, there was another group. It was a small but loud minority of women who continued to say with much injured innocence, "The dirt is in your own mind, boys. The ad simply asks a woman does she or doesn't she use haircoloring."

Noticing how the sexes were divided, I knew we had it made. We could count on all the men in the family reading the ads for sheer shock value like *Lolita* or *Fanny Hill* and getting the message in spite of themselves. And we had another even greater advantage with women. We realized that most of the women we wanted to influence had been brought up as I had been—to believe it wasn't quite nice to admit out loud that a nice girl ever got an off-color meaning about anything, especially in mixed company. Well, that's how it was in 1955.

With this in mind, it was pretty safe to challenge *Life* to research the ad among their women employees. It's hard to believe this now but they couldn't find one woman who admitted to getting a double meaning from the words, "Does she . . . or doesn't she?" This so knocked *Life*'s all-male panel for a loop that the advertising was accepted and everybody began to get rich —the hair color manufacturer, the space sellers, the typesetters, even the makers of dress fabrics pictured on the models. Haircoloring figures spiraled from about seven per cent of the woman population to way over fifty per cent.

An amusing sidelight. In October 1962, when *Time* (part of the *Time-Life* chain) ran a double-cover montage on the advertising industry, the only words featured, of the millions of words that had been written in advertising, was the slogan "Does she . . . or doesn't she?"

And thus a seemingly non-acceptable phrase turned a non-acceptable commodity into the highly respected industry that haircoloring is today. It must be that two negatives do make a positive. I would have liked it if George and his raised eyebrow were still around to see this.

As the client's advertising budget was going from about $400,000 or $500,000 to about $33 million a year, television was added. Commercials were cast in the same warm image as the mother and child print ads. Print ads and commercials that not only built fantastic sales profiles but won all kinds of awards all over the world. So well did the Miss Clairol campaign establish a personality—we even got letters from nuns lauding our mother and child—that movies have been reviewed as "a one-hour Miss Clairol commercial."

This may not be high praise for the film industry but it's a real nice feeling for the ad writer.

4

Why Not Try a Little Loving Care and See?

When I think of Clairol Loving Care, I always remember the time a British television station banned a series of our commercials on the ground that lead-off questions like "How long has it been since your husband asked you to dance?" or "How long has it been since your husband brought you flowers?" could be very disruptive of British family life.

This almost created an international incident between England and me.

In America, the "Does she . . . or doesn't she?" campaign had taken off like a rocket. Straight up. The product was good. The advertising was right. And millions of women were ready.

But that was for Miss Clairol permanent color, which requires a peroxide developer as it is euphemistically called, and doesn't go away until the hair grows out. What about all those women who hated gray hair but were afraid to commit themselves to anything permanent, who wanted all the benefits of using haircoloring without using haircoloring? A wistful hope.

In those days—and this was in 1962 or 1963—there were some products called rinses but the rinses really did nothing you could see except on your pillowcase, collar, or comb. However, there was acceptance for the word "rinse." Preliminary research had already shown us that even when a woman kept her head in a vat for hours she described the process as a rinse. And as for gray hair? We hardly ever found a woman with gray in her hair who didn't say that everyone in her family had grayed before twenty-five. So we concluded that, like middle age, which is always ten years older than you are now, gray hair seems premature at any age.

Loving Care was Clairol's new way to hide unwanted gray hair. It was more than a rinse in that you had to keep it on your head longer but it didn't rub off on your pillow or husband. It was less than a tint because it didn't use peroxide developer, so it couldn't change your real color, just shine it up. But it could color the gray, which is empty hair that has lost its pigment. And that was news!

And Loving Care was a cinch to use. You just poured it on your head from the bottle, sloshed it around a bit, waited a little, then rinsed it off. Like a rinse. There was no tiresome sectioning of hair and applying of color to each strand as in a tint done by a professional.

We needed an advertising idea that would appeal to this older, more conservative woman, that would combine all the ordinary familiarity and ease of the word "rinse" yet avoid the stigma of "dye," with the magic properties of a product that could single out the gray and color it to match.

Time was getting short. "Better dredge up a little something soon," I told my subconscious over and over but nothing much came to mind until one evening when I was brisking along toward home. Suddenly I became aware that I was singing what we used to call opera when I was a kid. My highest soprano was declaiming, "Hate that gray?" My basso profundo was answering, "Wash it away!" Soprano, "Hate that gray?" Basso, "Wash it away!"

As a rule, it is not my style to pace the streets of New York loudly singing duets with myself in two voices.

But this evening I had stepped back in time some thirty-five years and was repeating a pattern that hadn't surfaced since those Sunday mornings in Brooklyn when my sisters and I used to extemporize opera around the simplest routines of living.

My mother was an opera buff. She thought nothing of traveling an hour into Manhattan to the old Metropolitan Opera House. There she would stand on line for three to five hours for the privilege of buying a ticket that allowed her to stand inside for three more hours to hear her favorites: Caruso, Galli-Curci, Geraldine Farrar. She would bring home the arias, duets and quartets on Red Seal records which we played on our big wind-up Victrola. How dramatic they sounded in their original Italian or French. How mundane the words when we read them translated into English in the librettos, especially as combined with the wildly improbable plots outlined.

Sunday mornings in our house became a kind of bedlam that sounded something like this. Say, we were setting the table for lunch:

Me (high drama in high C):
    "Here's a napkin for your lapkin!
    A napkin for your lapkin!"
My sisters (in counterpoint):
    "Oh, a napkin for her lapkin, girl.
    Oh, a napkin for her lapkin, Shirl!"

Or if one of us was preparing for the morning ablutions, it might be:

Me (in bell-toned contralto):
    "I th-ink, I th-ink, I th-ink
    I'm going to wash my neck.
    Oh, heck, I have to wash my neck."
Lillian (simultaneously in double time. Soprano):
    "To wear your nice white sweater,
    I think that you had better . . ."
Ellenore (staccato. Bass):
    "Get the dreck off your neck."

Now here was I, some thirty-five years later, operatically washing the consumer's hair. My subconscious hadn't let me down. It had made the connection through the word "wash," a nice, safe, easy word never before associated with haircoloring and an adequate enough description of the "sloshing-through" process of Loving Care.

"Hate that gray? Wash it away!" How ridiculously simple. Almost too simple. It needed a touch of magic. We had it in the product. "Colors only the gray without changing your natural hair color." Here was magic indeed! How did Loving Care know which hair to color when it colored only the gray? I mean how *did* it know just *which* hair to color?

We found out later, of course, that it was the very sheerness of the product that accomplished the trick. The color just didn't show on hair that still retained its own color pigment.

Those lines plus some very reassuring, sweetly reasonable body text might have been enough to do the job but I felt the approach still lacked a sock to the emotions.

I also had qualms about limiting the appeal to women who had already admitted to themselves that they hated that gray. For big success, we'd have to expand the market to gather in all those ladies who had become stoically resigned to it. This could only be accomplished by reawakening whatever dissatisfactions they may have had when they first spotted it, not only as an assault to their vanity but for the ramifications that might be affecting other aspects of their lives.

So I added a small photo of a happily smiling, middle-aged man to the bottom of the ad with the caption: "Makes your husband feel younger too, just to look at you!"

You can see how this could practically turn the act of hair-coloring into a selfless little something one did for one's loved ones.

The husband line was a natural for T.V. dramatizations and I had no doubts about its working because I had been brought up to believe a husband's approval makes the world go round for most women. That's the way it was in my mother's home and in my own home too. That's the way I thought it was all over. I guess I really believe all those schmaltzy things I say in the ads. It seems to have nothing to do with the hardheaded strategies I can work out for marketing products.

In the early sixties the soap opera was not only having its way with daytime television, it was threatening to invade prime evening time, which it subsequently did via *Peyton Place*. We decided to do fifty-eight-second soap operas, seriously, without organ music, in the hope that they would magnetize the viewer to identify with the heroine. Isn't that the goal of all soap operas? A photoscript of one of these ads appears in the photo insert.

Other commercials, all in the same format, led off with "How long has it been since your husband brought you flowers?" "How long has it been since your husband asked you *out* to dinner?" and similar questions followed by the lines "Maybe gray hair makes you seem older than you are. Hate that gray? . . . etc." All designed to latch onto little dissatisfactions in the average viewer's bosom. They were really problem/solution commercials, very right for their era, and Loving Care soared away to top billings. Maybe the concern of the British about the ads' ability to disrupt family life was not without validity. They ran them eventually, but not until they had lopped off the arresting questions in the first twenty seconds. England's Loving Care commercials started at the line, "Hate that gray?"

However, in America, the commercials ran for years just the way I wrote them and we got letters from many women, telling us how much the quality of their lives had improved in some small way or other, after they had washed away the gray. It could be that they liked their looks better so their dispositions improved. Like the song says, "You've got to have a dream, you've got to have a hope." One could begin to feel like a do-gooder.

I think I was in my teens when it dawned on me that my father was not a rich man. I don't know how much money he made but it couldn't have been a lot. He bought neckties in quantity on consignment from manufacturers, then sold and delivered them to neighborhood momma and poppa stores in an era when large chain and department stores were beginning to encroach on small retailers. My father enjoyed visiting with the storekeepers. He was an interesting, learned man with a wry, dry sense of humor. And they looked forward to his visits.

But it was the way my mother managed the money that worked the magic. We always had great things to eat in the stove or icebox. It was never a problem to get kids to come play at our house after school. Sometimes we had to run or skip all the way home, so impatient were they to encounter the delicious smells of cooking, the sweet, fresh scent of cakes baking that greeted us as we opened the door. And she was generous with the portions. She understood that, for a child, the very act of eating something delicious can turn plain play into a party.

And the way she could sew and embroider! She not only made all our clothes, even our coats, from her own patterns, she did tasteful inventive things with doilies and curtains and slipcovers for the house. My mother had golden hands. I remember how often her friends used to say, "Rose, you have golden hands."

It wasn't until my sister Lillian and I went to high school, Girls' High School in Brooklyn, that we realized there were girls whose mothers had never sewed a stitch. Girls who wore expensive ready-mades from elegant New York stores. One girl especially, whom we called Scarlet Fever because her complexion was always so flushed, lived in a big white mansion with two-story pillars, set on about a half block of prime Brooklyn real estate. Years later, when I saw *Gone With the Wind*, it came to me that the camera crew could have gone on location in Flatbush to Scarlet Fever's house for Scarlett O'Hara's Tara.

One of the reasons my parents had insisted on an all-girls' high school instead of Erasmus Hall, which was closer but co-ed, was that we wouldn't need silk stockings. They felt we'd stay content in cotton ones if there were no boys around to show off our legs to. Little did they know that we were about to join the flapper generation.

The flapper look, as uniform for teen-agers as jeans and attic clothes are today, was a short two-piece, long-sleeved, dark wool jersey dress with white linen Peter Pan collar and cuffs called a Bramley. (Franklin Simon was the original source, but the style was soon ripped off by other retailers.) This little number was worn with wildly plaided argyll wool stockings which cost seven dollars a pair (silk stockings were only about two dollars then) and heavy brogue oxfords with fringed flaps obtainable only in boys' shoe departments. When it rained or snowed, galoshes covered the brogues. They were worn unhooked, turned down, and they flapped when one walked. The walk was distinctive too. Instead of putting one foot down in front of the other, one strode widely to the side with large hip-swinging steps. You didn't make much head-on progress that way but two flappers side-striding in unison could hip-swing the ordinary walker right off into the gutter.

The flapper overcoat was usually a heavy herringbone tweed with swinging back and breast pockets to keep your hands in and your elbows akimbo as you swaggered. And the hat that completed the picture was a rolled-up felt sailor called a Piping Rock.

For a short time it was important to edge the brim of one's hat with little round brass paper clips called Shifter pins. This proclaimed to the world that you were a member in good standing of a secret society called The Shifters. Being a Shifter meant that you had been conned into paying fifteen or twenty cents for about five of these little brass paper clips and could, in turn, induct another classmate to get back your investment. Somehow, this never came off. The truly enterprising one was the founding Shifter. Having invented the society, she blitzed the class by buying out all the brass paper clips available at the local stationery store. They came in little round cardboard boxes, a hundred for a nickel.

The connection seems a little hazy now, but I believe this is the reason why I've never taken part in a chain letter promising me a fortune in cash.

My sister and I were ready with the Shifter pins but we still didn't have the hats to clip them on until one Saturday morning when my mother announced that we were all going shopping. She'd had a long conference with my father. Now, she said, she was prepared to take her hand off her heart, put the sewing machine away, and go for the complete flapper ensemble for her girls. And she did! She went all the way, even to the ultimate accessory, a banjo-ukulele with bright-colored ribbons attached to the keys.

The ukulele was a real sacrifice. It not only entailed lessons for two girls, but it meant that our house, usually pervaded by philharmonic and operatic sounds, now rang with the wild cries of Ukulele Ike. My mother tactfully broke those records when dusting but we managed to replace them through canny manipulation of our school allowances.

But we were not insensitive to the financial strain on the family budget. It was at the end of my first year in high school that I decided, as the "boy" in the family, it was up to me to get a job and *fardeen* a little during the coming summer vacation.

The New York *Times* had several large want ads for file clerks, mostly placed by large insurance companies located on Maiden Lane in downtown Manhattan. That sounded like an exciting neighborhood and since I had no trained skill it seemed to me that filing would be exactly right for a first job.

I planned to get there early before the crowd, like eight in the morning, but when I got there at least twenty girls were ahead of me, all busily filling out applications. I took one. Name, address, age, previous experience, religion. Name and address was easy. Age? I was not quite thirteen but I had been pushed ahead a year and a half in grammar school and I was tall and developed so I thought I could get away with sixteen. Experience? If I'd just left school, how could I have experience, so I put down, None. Religion? Jewish.

I was prepared to wait about an hour but suddenly I noticed that the woman in charge was beckoning me to approach her desk.

"I think Mr. Smyth would like to see you next," she said with an encouraging smile.

A surge of happiness went through me. I was glad that I had worn my neat brown dress with the neat white collar and the neat Windsor bow like it said in the little "How to . . ." books.

She took my application, glanced at it, and suddenly I became aware that I was being dismissed.

"I'm sorry," she said coldly, as she beckoned to another girl, "but all the filing jobs are filled."

I wanted to cry. It was my first turndown. She had seemed so friendly, I just couldn't understand the sudden change.

Walking toward the elevators, I saw a ladies' room. I went in to blow my nose and repair whatever damages the welling tears had made. As I stood looking in the mirror, the girl who was called after me came in.

"Gee, I got the job," she said with a big smile.

"Doing what?" I asked.

"Filing. They're hiring a load of 'em."

"I wonder why she didn't take me?" I said.

She studied my face a moment.

"What's your name?"

"Polykoff. Shirley Polykoff."

She looked down.

"They never hire Jews. None of these places."

"Why not?" I asked. It was in the middle twenties.

She shrugged her shoulders.

"How should I know?"

"Thanks," I said.

Now I was mad. And a little scared too, as I decided to answer
the other ad in my pocket. That company was located in the very
next building. The So-and-so Underwriters of America. They all
used such high-sounding, patriotic names.

I took a job application form. Name? Shirley Miller. I don't
think Miller sounds all that Aryan but it was the name on the
desk of the interviewer. Age? Sixteen. Religion? Christian Science.
The only thing I knew about Christian Science was that they
didn't believe in medicine or doctors. They left their healing to
Jesus Christ. In those days, I was even frightened to pronounce
the words "Jesus Christ." I thought my own God would strike me
dead. But I knew even less about other religions so I converted
on the spot to Christian Science.

I got the job. Eleven dollars a week. And that was the start of
Shirley Miller's sad but meteoric ten-week rise in the insurance
industry.

I had been interviewed by a steely-faced, steely-haired man
with steel-rimmed glasses. He had nice smily eyes when you looked
directly at him but I was afraid to look directly at him for fear
he'd read the lies in my face.

"You look like a smart girl," he said. "How come you're not
finishing high school? Let's see"—he looked at my application—
"you only have a year to go." I had put myself down as a junior.

"We need the money," I said sadly. "I intend to do the last
year in night school. I promised my father."

He smiled approvingly and then looked at me searchingly.

"Are you sure this isn't just a summer job? You know, we don't
like to train people and then have them leave after a few weeks."

"Oh no, no, no," I said, crossing my fingers in my lap. "I want
to make good at this. I have to help out at home."

It got to him.

I felt terrible. We had been brought up not to do two things.
One was not to tattle. You couldn't say to my father, "Poppa,
guess what Lillian did?" because he'd always answer, "If Lillian
wants me to know, she'll tell me herself." And the other was not to
lie. Lying was simply inexcusable. Nothing could mitigate the
offense of telling a lie. It was hard to hold my head up. But I did
well on the job.

At the end of two weeks the personnel man sent for me.

"Miss Miller," he said, "we find your work very satisfactory indeed. Neat and quick and accurate too. It's true, you've only been here two weeks, but we believe in encouraging initiative. As of today, you will receive a two-dollar raise. Look for thirteen dollars in your next pay envelope."

The *fardeener* in me was proud. The rest of me felt awful. I was so worried about giving myself away through some unknowing comment that I tried to avoid socializing with my fellow workers. They construed this, I found out later, as evidence of trouble at home. Possibly between my mother and father. One girl even guessed that my mother might be Catholic and my father Protestant "and that always creates a lot of strife in a family."

The first week in August, I got another two-dollar raise. I was now *fardeening* fifteen dollars a week. There were only four more weeks till school started. How would I ever tell the personnel man, who these days went out of his way to smile at me, that I had to leave? He might see through me and discover I was a liar. Lying would be added to the sins of the Jews. And I would have been responsible. I decided to say I was leaving town. The family was moving to Philadelphia. My uncle had a job for me in his own business.

I was summoned to the personnel office.

"Ahhh, Miss Miller," said the personnel man. "You're leaving us for Philadelphia? Will you be going back to school?"

"Oh no, no," I said, thinking of this as a trap question. "My mother's brother lives in Philadelphia. I'll be working for him. And maybe now I will get to night school."

"Here, Miss Miller," he said, handing me a large white envelope. "I have written a letter of recommendation to our Philadelphia branch of Underwriters. If your uncle's job doesn't work out, this will help you get a fine job. Possibly even a supervisor's."

I wanted to stick my tongue out at him and say, "You see? You see? You're all wrong about Jews," but it stuck in my throat. I felt ashamed that I couldn't get it out and even more ashamed to confess my deception.

I felt the same way during the good-bys to my fellow workers. Some of the boys and girls wanted my new address. They had relatives in Philadelphia and sometimes even visited there. So I promised again and again to write.

I expected to feel joyously released-at-last when I walked out that final day, but I didn't. Even after two weeks in school, I was still moping around worrying that if I didn't write as promised the insurance company people would somehow guess that I had lied and hadn't moved to Philadelphia at all. I hated the fact that the fear of being found out seemed more heinous than the crime itself. I owed it to my people to write. I experimented with faking the Philadelphia postmark but then I'd have to hand-deliver all the cards. And that was just not possible.

So the following Tuesday, telling only my sister Lillian, I played hooky from school, took the hour-long ride to Penn Station, and there boarded a railroad train to Philadelphia. In the Philadelphia terminal, I found Philadelphia scenic postcards, addressed them to key people in my department, made up a special message for the personnel man, signed them all Shirley Miller, then mailed them back to New York City.

After an hour wait on the platform, I caught a northbound train back to New York, which took another two hours, and the subway on to Brooklyn. When I got home it was very late and I had missed supper. My sisters were already in bed but my father was waiting for me in the dining room.

"I know you have been to Philadelphia," he said sternly. "That's all your sister would tell me. So you'll please be kind enough to say why you dared to go there alone. On a school day. And without asking your mother."

I edged into the room so the table could be between me and my father. Our dining room was typical of the time. Crowded against the walls were the extra chairs, two matching chests, a highboy and a lowboy, and a tall crystal closet that displayed all the sparkling cut glass pieces my father had picked up for my mother through the years. In the center of the room, under a Tiffany-type chandelier, was a large round table surrounded by space for passage. We kids had learned to use that space strategically. My father had a quick temper that flashed up furiously, then faded like summer lightning. We discovered fairly early that he wouldn't chase around the table because it wasn't dignified not to be able to catch us. And he was a man of dignity.

"Poppa," I said, carefully measuring out the space between us, "I'll tell you all about it but please don't get mad until I finish."

And then it all tumbled out. With my head down, I told him about the initial turndown. About the change of name for the second interview. The lies about religion. The raises I had earned that made it all seem even more unfair.

Suddenly I heard an odd sound. I had never seen my father cry. Nor am I sure that he did then, but he jumped up, brushed by me with a pat on the head, and went into the bathroom and locked the door.

"Your father has a cold," my mother said. "Come, it's late. I'll give you some supper and you'll go to bed."

As I was falling asleep, I heard my father come into the room.

"You're sleeping?" he said softly.

"No, Poppa."

He rumpled my hair. "It's a little early for you to learn this, but some money is too expensive."

As he went into his own room, I heard my mother say, "Ach, that anti-Semitism. It's the curse of the Jews."

"Not *of* the Jews, Momma," he answered, "*on* the Jews."

I felt very warm and close to my father that night. I think it was the first time I began to see him as a man instead of just as a father, to be aware of all the contradictions of his personality. He seemed so compassionate and understanding, yet I knew him to be quite closed off at other times. He was painfully shy and introspective and awkward in his actions, yet he could be bold and arrogant or quite gracious and rather gallant when we least expected it. He didn't talk much except on those occasions when Lillian and I had boys over and then it seemed to us that he talked too much. But he must have been interesting because they said they enjoyed those conversations. Maybe because he spoke to them as equals. Sometimes I'd get so sleepy listening, I'd go into the kitchen, open the windows, and do deep breathing and some stretching exercises just to keep awake.

My mother thought mealtimes were a great time for family conversations but he always had his head in a book or newspaper even when he was eating. My mother strongly disapproved of this and once she even switched the creamer and sugar bowl from their accustomed positions on the table. When he reached for the sugar over his paper and dipped his fingers in the cream instead, we all laughed but he laughed too, so nothing changed.

And he was very authoritarian. I remember how often in our day-to-day transactions we used to tell him, "Poppa, you're a man of few words. And most of them are no."

However, on those milestones in his life, like when we graduated from high school or at his first grandson's Bar Mitzvah, or on his own fiftieth wedding anniversary, he made little speeches that were beautiful expressions of how he felt about us all: gracefully phrased, sparked with great humor that revealed the man he might have been all of the time had conditions been a little less harassing. He could make jokes, literate, whimsical jokes (that is, when he made them), about almost anything except his own irascibility, which he hated in himself but seemed unable to control. We feared these quick, violent flashes of temper and it is only now, when I look back, that I realize that when any child broke a rule of the house my mother, in reporting the facts to him, made sure the erring one was out of reach on the opposite side of that round dining-room table and she always managed to station herself close enough to catch his arm, if ever it was raised to strike. Not so much to save us pain as to save him from the pain and humiliation he felt for himself on the times he had connected with one of us.

My mother, on the other hand, had good humor but no sense of humor. That is, she could take a joke but couldn't make a joke. But it was her enjoyment and zest for life that colored every inch of our living. And because my father was so taciturn, she encouraged us kids to babble. I must have sensed this need in her because she says I used to start telling her about what happened in school each day when I was still down at the street corner. And didn't really stop telling until she put out the afternoon hot cocoa and home-baked yeast cake. We weren't allowed to talk with our mouths full, so for a while there would be quiet. We kids had two ploys in the snack department. One was to eat the cake fast and drink the cocoa slowly so we could get more cake and have it come out even. The other was to drink off half the cocoa and then stuff the cup with all the cake it could take. This was called mak-

ing an ice cream soda and the delicious mess was not drunk but
eaten with a spoon.

Neither my mother nor my father was particularly demonstrative
with each other or with us. It was only with Ellenore, who was six
years younger, that my father showed any outward affection. She
was the only child he ever picked up or fondled. As the baby, she
got most of the attention and, as she is wont to say, most of the
bossing around.

The word "love" itself was not used often in our home. It was
an awesome, committing word reserved for the time we'd "fall in
love." Yet I do know that our home and family life had a great
deal of affection in it—warmth, closeness, and especially respect.
It was in the atmosphere. It was in the way my father spoke of
and to my mother. He loved the way she cared for him and reminded him to eat. The way she put herself out to entertain his
snooty relatives who, she said, held their heads so high they looked
as though they had "fleas up their nose." They were an older
generation who had come to America years before my parents and
already had in the family one doctor and one schoolteacher daughter married to a dentist. Her preparations for their entertainment
made it look as though my father's necktie business was part of
the gold one found in the streets of America.

It was in the way my mother dressed up for my father. And for
us too. He used to say on those rare occasions, "I don't know anything much about cards but I do know that I hold four queens
and all of them are aces."

I can't remember ever seeing my mother with her hair un-
combed. We knew she used curlers to set her hair but we never
saw them on her head. We never saw her in a dirty or torn wrap-
per. No matter how early in the morning, her house dress was always fresh and clean and neatly pressed. Her skin was always
clear and smooth. Her blonde hair shiny. It wasn't that she was
vain, though I can see now that she was. It was more because she
believed (and she taught us this) that if we loved to look at nice
things we must ourselves be nice to look at. That if we enjoyed
beautiful scenery we must believe that other people did too and
that it was incumbent on us to keep the environment as lovely
as possible. So my father kept the outside as well as the inside of
our house painted and the cellar scrupulously clean while my

mother kept the small garden manicured and bright with flowers. Even today, at ninety-three, I have never caught her unaware of herself, her appearance, or current politics. My father always accepted this as a compliment to himself. And in a way it was.

I always remember this and maybe that's why it was easy for me to take Loving Care into its second phase. In 1968 we ran three-page gate-folds in magazines. Loving Care, as you remember, "colored only the gray without changing your natural hair color."

Page one: (Husband reading newspaper at breakfast. Wife looking neglected. Hair streaky gray.) Caption: "What would your husband do if suddenly you looked ten years younger?" Small type: "Turn the page and see." Followed by a two-page spread showing husband with wife cradled in his arms. Her hair now all shiny brown with no trace of gray. Both are laughing joyously, lasciviously. Caption: "Try a little Loving Care and see!"

It worked.

5

Pardon Me While I Take off My Coonskin Cap

It seems to me that, next to a slow lingering corrosive death from a dreadful sickness, the greatest indignity that can happen to a human being is not being able to get a job because the economy has closed him out. We see a lot of this today when fully trained, able men and women in their late forties and early fifties are let go because of a tightening of industry finances. Suddenly all doors in their chosen work are closed to them, mostly because of their age, an age long touted in song and story as the best years of one's life.

The Great Depression during the decade of the thirties, however, was very democratic. It included all age groups. No class was left out. Whether it was Harvard '32 or N.Y.U., Erasmus Hall High School or P.S. 153, thousands of bright young capable people were being pushed out into a world where there was no place for them to go but on some long queue for a handout or a WPA job if they were lucky. All over the city you could see strong young bodies with heads down alongside the apathetic old ones, shoveling snow or raking leaves depending on the season. And the most unlikely persons selling apples. If there is any truth in the doctor-apple tie-in, I should stay healthy for years to come, I ate so many apples. Five cents apiece. I could afford it because I had a job

writing advertising copy for the Peck Advertising Agency on Bab-O
and the I. J. Fox fur account.

I. J. Fox was a very interesting man, single-minded and energy-
packed. As legend had it, he had come out of the First World War
to be a streetcar conductor, saved his nickels until he had enough
money to buy one fur coat wholesale, then advertised it in the
Personals column as a "must move to warm climate, almost new
fur coat at sacrifice" item. This may be apocryphal but it seems
that he continued to pile up single sales like this until he had
enough money to open a store on Sixth Avenue. He had just completed the move onward and upward to Fifth Avenue, to a beautiful nine-floor emporium, when I was hired by the agency.

Mr. Fox, or I.J. as he preferred to be called, believed in advertising. He was one of the first retailers to be on radio with a
small singing-playing combo called the Fox Fur Trappers who carried on incidental conversation between song numbers in a kind
of French-Canadian English dialect. I had to write at least eight
or ten commercials a week and got so caught up in their patois
that I had to say to myself, "Pardon me while I take off my coon-
skin cap," to come back to reality.

After a few years, when we were photographing famous Hollywood stars wearing I. J. Fox fur coats and fur-trimmed cloth
coats, we got Irene Bordoni, the international French actress who
had just finished a movie in California, to do the commercials.
She used to complain that the French-accented pidgin English
that I wrote for her made her sound like an ignorant French
peasant instead of the cultured woman that she was. And knowing absolutely nothing about the subject except what I had
learned from French comedians in vaudeville, I helped override
her objections by insisting there wasn't much point in having an
Irene Bordoni unless she spoke English with the kind of French
accent Americans expect. It was French like the Russian I remember from a Robert W. Chambers' novel that I had read as a
kid where an American caught in Russia tries to make himself understood by saying, "What the devilovitch is the mattsky?"

But the daily newspaper ads for I. J. Fox presented the biggest
challenge. Every other month we had an event. An Anniversary
Toast with fur-coated models rising out of champagne glasses, a
Birthday Salute with cake and candles, a Whale-of-a-Sale, a Feb-

ruary Clearance, a June Close-out. And when all else failed, we'd photograph Mr. I. J. Fox knee-deep in furs "scouring the markets of the world" or "combing the four corners of the earth for the finest pelts at never-before savings." It seems the earth was very square during the Depression. Also cleaned and combed. And the merchandise never anything but hand-picked.

One summer, when he went abroad for two weeks, I had to write an I. J. Fox ad listing some hot bargains in fur coats. It was scheduled to run in the English edition of the Paris *Herald Trib-une* while he was in France and he wanted the headline to read, "Welcome Americans in Paris." I protested the word "welcome" and suggested that the word "greetings" might be more appro-priate since the Americans we were welcoming were mostly American expatriates who had been living there for years. (Dur-ing the twenties and early thirties, the French exchange was very kind to the American dollar.) But he said he hated "nit-pick-ing over words" and liked the warmth in the word "welcome," so the headline stayed. He was the kind of man who could welcome you to your own flat and even encourage you to feel at home there and not seem out of order.

Mr. Fox was one of the first to use skywriting. Over Manhat-tan, mind you, and in letters miles high. During the summer it was personally very satisfying to me to lie on the beach and watch the name of I. J. Fox float by in the sky.

At this time of year our store windows featured little tableaux of elegantly dressed moths at dinner parties dining on fine furs, ex-claiming over their tastiness. And in the newspapers we ran fur storage ads showing a woman with her mouth open registering horror as a moth flew out of her closet. These were called "Oh, my God" pictures. Even today, in my climate-sealed apartment, when I open a summer closet I still get that old "Oh, my God" feeling. Not because I expect to see a moth fly out but because the smell of moth preventative is enough to knock one over—it's what my youngest granddaughter calls "Gammy's summer o-dure."

Mr. Fox liked a certain kind of earnest writing in his ads. What I called my high school oratorical prose. Very sincere and over-blown. My experience in this style of writing went all the way back to my junior year in high school.

We were having general school elections and one of the girls nominated for president of the General Organization was Sally Hudson. She was a tall, slim, quiet blonde with better-than-average scholastic and athletic abilities. I had just won the district high school oratorical contest and been elected to the Dramatic Society. My secret dreams saw me as a serious, convincing writer and speaker with a brilliant future in dramatic acting, so when Sally asked me to make her nomination speech, I accepted with enthusiasm. The speech I prepared for Sally's nomination at the school assembly was full of enthusiasm, too. Very sincere, studded with ringing clichés and what later became known as Shirley exaggerations. At that time politicians were still using corny phrases like "from the rock-bound coast of Maine to the Golden Gate of Frisco" in the national convention halls and I lifted an actual portion of a real nomination speech which I altered to suit, paraphrasing the most colorful portions, adding a hyperbole here and there to describe Sally's unique capabilities to govern the General Organization of Girls' High School.

My manner of delivery was most serious. In fact I was so nervous I couldn't touch the lectern on the platform for fear of shaking all my notes off to the floor. When I finished my first sentence there was a titter. At the end of the second sentence the audience laughed out loud. And the further I went on, the more uproarious they became. I didn't know what was happening to me but I couldn't quit and continued on with this very exaggerated, humorless speech, which wound up with a cheer, complete with swinging arms:

> "Viva, viva, viva vest!
> Who is the one who could lead us best?
> Sally Hudson! Sally Hudson!
> A grand girl. A great leader! Your next president!"

The assembly hall hooted and cheered. Soon girls were running up to the platform, patting me on the back, throwing their arms around my shoulders. Sally Hudson was elected and I got a reputation as a satirist and wit because of my great spoof on the whole business of election speeches. Never until now has it been revealed that I really meant every word of it. I was more than a little bruised inside but I never let on. Nor did I achieve any objectivity or perspective on the matter until later that year when I read "Merton of the Movies" in the *Saturday Evening Post*.

Merton, as you may or may not recall, is a young humorless fellow who goes to Hollywood to make his mark as a great tragic actor. From the first film test, his alert directors discover that the more seriously Merton takes himself and his acting the more hilarious he appears on the screen. The whole idea then becomes one of keeping this aspect of his acting a secret from him. The climax comes at the premiere of his first movie. He goes prepared to view himself in a serious dramatic triumph only to discover to soul-shattering effect that he is a straight-faced, sad-faced comic of the Musty Suffa variety. I shouldn't say variety because Musty Suffa was unique in the two-reel flicks in the days before Buster Keaton and Laurel and Hardy.

Sheepishly, I made the connection to Merton and it helped cool my burning humiliation. But, more important, it was a lesson in how to temper my natural enthusiasm to reality. I was sold on Sally, so I had played it to the hilt. Never again, I promised myself, would I go over the hilt.

However, the trap remains. Even today I find it almost impossible to write about something I don't believe in. So I do not rest until I've discovered some quality, some aspect of the product —no matter how slight or fragile—that will prove irresistible to me and thus to the consumer. But I have to sell myself first even if it requires hypnotizing myself through a Shirley exaggeration. And the more earnest and enthusiastic I become about the product the more watchful I am to limit my oratory. (I write my copy out loud.) It is this blend of overwriting and toning down that I've always called the Merton Mix.

The Merton Mix was effective in bringing in the customers to I. J. Fox all during the Depression. And they did get bargains. I verified this myself by touring the department stores from 32nd Street to 59th Street. Mr. Fox had everything they had—from the most moderately priced furs and cloth coats at Macy's and Gimbel's to the most luxurious coats at Bergdorf or Bonwit Teller, and because of the great volume of his operation they actually were fifteen to a hundred dollars cheaper, depending on the price range. That's a lot of money to save at any time but it was especially appreciated during that desperate economy. So I went along writing earnest, sincere ads for radio which toward the end of my tenure with Fox had as its musical theme a song he had purchased from a friend:

> Love-ly lay-dee. Love-ly laydee,
> In your coat of I. J. Fox mink
> You are looking dee-vine.
> Lo-v-ly laydee from above,
> Let me speak my love for you-oo.

And earnest, sincere newspaper ads with such slogans as "Son of a furrier, Grandson of a furrier, three generations of fur experience"; "Nine floors devoted exclusively to furs"; "I. J. Fox, not Jack-of-all-trades but master of one—furs!" Heavy ads all pointing up his heavy specialization in furs. And after a while I stopped wondering why it had been so terribly important for the agency to seek out a copywriter with a light touch for the job and stopped bemoaning the loss of my hard-earned department store reputation for apt, catchy headlines. Not only because I suddenly began to realize how lucky I was to be making all that money when so many bright people were out of work but because I instinctively began to recognize that Mr. Fox's insistence on immediate response to his advertising was invaluable training for any kind of ad writing. It didn't matter to Mr. Fox if it rained or snowed or sleeted or if all means of transportation were halted. If the women didn't throng into the store first thing in the morning, the campaign was a failure and we'd start all over again. This could mean working around the clock. It became a matter of self-preservation to "bring 'em down to 36th Street" before nine-thirty. Where else but in retail advertising can one so quickly see the effectiveness of one's work? It's the best experience a copywriter can get.

It was during these early days of the Depression that I met George. My office was on Madison Avenue near 40th Street and his office was on 40th Street near Madison Avenue and the inevitable coffee shop was somewhere in between.

He used to see me, I learned later, a couple of mornings a week having breakfast in that coffee shop. With six or eight men. Never less than three. This made a strong unfavorable impression on him. Who did I think I was? Some movie queen? A musical comedy star walking slowly down the steps toward eight dinner-jacketed men singing, "Oh, Kay, you're okay with me?" His was a lively imagination. But then, how could he know that they were just fellow workers, writers and art directors from the agency, that there were no other women on the staff and that it was only after my horoscope had been thoroughly explored in depth that I had been rather grudgingly welcomed to the all-male breakfast-lunch bunch?

To George, it was obvious from the way I comported myself that I thought I was pretty special. (As a bachelor, he fancied himself an expert in reading girls' expressions.) This became a personal challenge to him—so much so that he decided that, if ever he should meet me, he would teach me that I wasn't really all that special. This could become a lifetime project.

I never knew any of this until after we were married because I never saw George in the coffee shop. Six or eight men, especially when you're not committed to any one of them and your horoscope has promised warm, passionate friendships, can generate a lot of attention for a girl.

Fortunately, George and I did meet by chance at a New Year's Eve party in a place called Red Oaks near Rumson, New Jersey. This was a kind of paying club in the country run by a wonderful old family named Strunsky from Washington Square in Greenwich Village. One of their daughters was Leanore, who was married to Ira Gershwin. Ira and George Gershwin were just at the beginning of their fabulous achievements and were surrounded by equally fine struggling talents who were to make it later in music, painting, literature, on Broadway, in Hollywood, and all over the world. In that group I had a certain distinction too. I was the only writer who made money every week—regularly.

I was just past twenty-five at the time and, according to Brooklyn standards in those days, I was well on my way to being an old maid. I have since reflected that what seems like an old maid to one generation can become a child bride in the next. I had been seeing two fellows on a fairly regular basis and, while we had great affection for each other and they are still my friends, there was no electricity, not even a touch of heartache in the even pattern of our relationships. But 1932 was the year of the Polykoff.

Suddenly, every man I met seemed mad to marry me, so it is not surprising that when George walked in and stopped short, dumbstruck by my presence, I didn't know that it was because he recognized me from the coffee shop. I interpreted it as simple evidence of another conquest and, turning to a friend, remarked, "Let's put another scalp on the belt!" Nor did I act humbly grateful for the fact that George and his friend Stanley spent most of the weekend plying me with small attentions. They left earlier than I did and when George said good-by he promised to call me. But two months went by and he didn't. I found out later that it was his way of showing me that I wasn't all that special. He felt he wasn't taking any chances because he knew he could always accidentally bump into me in the coffee shop. But I was still oblivious to all of that.

Then one morning (I remember the day because it was the big I. J. Fox Spring Fashion Show) George sent roses to my office. I was surprised to see his name on the enclosed card because in the rush of that particular season I hadn't given him much thought. I already knew he was a lawyer but I learned from the card that he was a partner in his firm and that his office was barely half a block away. On the back of the card, he asked me if I would call him for a date and supplied his phone number. In those days, self-respecting girls did not call fellows. "Darn him," I thought, "why do you have to do that!"

I looked at the roses. They were stupendous. The most dramatic I'd ever seen. Large dark red velvet on thick long thorny stems that kept pricking my fingers as I arranged them in a vase. "Is this some kind of message?" I grumbled as I sucked the blood from my thumb.

I decided I'd better put George and his roses out of my mind for the time being or I'd be late to I. J. Fox. I got there at ten in the morning and you could see from the number of women already milling around outside that the event was going to be an enormous success. The first show was scheduled for twelve and the repeat at three. I had helped plan the show. The agency had arranged for well-known movie stars to do the modeling. (In those days you got them for free just by mentioning their next picture in a corner of your ad.) I'd written the scripts for the fashions to be shown, written the invitations and the newspaper ads, and suddenly we were calling the police to come down and keep the ladies from breaking through the plate glass doors.

But the headiest part of all was to look out of our upstairs windows and see the people from Russeks, the big competition across the street, crowded around their executive windows watching what was happening as a direct result of *my* advertising. Carried away by the excitement of the achievement, I drank a toast to myself from the champagne punch bowl, especially mixed for the occasion from an old army recipe by Mr. I. J. Fox himself. A drink called Black Velvet after a smooth-running army horse with a legendary kick.

I liked the taste so I had another. And I guess still another. I had been carrying on a casual flirtation with the announcer. He was the famous "Time marches *on!*" voice of the old newsreels and used to moonlight for Mr. Fox under the name Hugh Conrad.

"Hey, I didn't know you drink," said Hugh.

"Neither did I," said I coyly over my shoulder.

Thus encouraged, he started chasing me around the racks of fur coats. Round and round we ran. I barely eluded him to the stairs. We were at the top of that nine-floor emporium and I think I finally emerged on the second with Hugh in hot pursuit. Fortunately, it was by now after hours, so the group I leaped into shouting, "Save me! Save me!" was composed of friends, that is, agency people and Fox personnel.

"Shhhh! For God's sake, shhhh!" said Mr. Peck, my boss, taking in the full flush of my beaming face. Then, turning to Conrad, "Please take her home. Please, will you take her home?"

"Brooklyn?" asked Conrad with disbelief.

Mr. Peck turned impatiently to an account man. "Well, get her back to the office then. Just get her out of here before she does something crazy."

Thus ended my flirtation with Hugh Conrad but it didn't calm me down. They got me back to the office somehow. I don't remember any part of that but I do remember that I was at an all-time high, making an awful racket about "Police on horses" and "horses on people." If someone tried to quiet me, I'd begin to weep. "No one to share the joy in my triumph," until one of the writers got so riled up, he started shouting too.

"I can't stand it. I tell you, I can't stand it. I'll take her home myself."

"No," said the secretary, "your wife will have a fit. Let's call one of her boy friends."

"Which boy friend?"

"What about this flower guy? Here, look, there's a card in the flowers.

She read George's number and dialed it.

"If you're a friend of Shirley Polykoff," she said when he got on the line, "you'd better come and get her. Oh, nothing serious . . ." She smiled sweetly at me as she continued into the phone, "She's had a triumph and she needs someone to share it with."

And that's how George met me the second time. Drunk.

He appeared at my office looking very proper and legal and quietly and efficiently gathered me up as though picking up drunken ladies was a usual part of his day. A taxi took us down to his apartment in Washington Square. By this time I was very docile and feeling awfully sick. In those days, if a lady accompanied a gentleman to his apartment, she was no lady, and I felt like a fallen woman in every sense of the word.

But George's intentions were entirely honorable. All he wanted to do was to call a doctor, which he did. The doctor came with sedatives and a stomach pump. Drastic measures for a few drinks but this doctor didn't fool around.

In the taxi going home to Brooklyn, I felt terribly ashamed and humbled and chastened and very grateful to George for his kindness and understanding while I mentally noted that he never once complained about the tedious taxi trip all the way to Brooklyn. "What a sport," I thought.

When we got to my home, he told the taxi to wait while he took my keys and opened the door.

"I hardly know you," I said as he turned to go. And then with a feeble attempt at humor, "But you know me inside and out. Will I see you again?"

"Tomorrow," he said.

He told me later that he took the taxi to the nearest subway. He could see from the meter that he had practically exhausted his funds.

I saw him for lunch and dinner the next day. And the next day and the next. And always, at the end of the evening, he taxied me to Brooklyn without a murmur or complaint.

The first week I knew him I was swept off my feet by his wide-ranging literary tastes and intellectual sophistication and by his seemingly limitless, vast connoisseurship of fascinating little out-of-the-way places all over England and Italy and especially in the provinces of France. Where to dine, what to order, and the right wines to accompany each *spécialité de la maison.*

"Gosh, he's been everywhere," I thought.

The second week I found out he did all of his traveling on Sundays through the New York *Times* Resort and Travel section and that his knowledge of fine wines was largely theoretical. But his own phrasing definitely had the elegance and bite of an H. L. Mencken and the unexpected element of surprise in an O'Henry short story. The intellectual sophistication was genuine—he was totally self-taught, having received his law degree at a time when a college degree was not a prerequisite. He attended N.Y.U. Law at night and loaded crates on trucks for R. H. Macy during the day. Sometime in between the two shifts, he read voraciously every book he could get at the Village Bookstore in Washington Square.

At the beginning of the third week we bought a car together. It was a brand-new Plymouth roadster with a convertible top and a rumble seat that cost a little over $650. At the end of the third week we drove to Reading, Pa., where I met his family for the first time and joined them in the Passover dinner celebration.

At the beginning of the fourth week, when I met him for lunch that Monday, he said out of a clear sky, "Polly" (the business of the name Polly comes up again more pertinently in a later chapter), "Polly, I'm sorry I can't marry you."

"I didn't know you'd asked me," I said.

"Didn't I?" he said, brushing it aside. "I must have."

"Well, you didn't, but it's all right," I said brightly though the room seemed to reel a bit. "But as it doesn't seem to matter now, may I ask why?"

"Because everybody, well, it seems like everybody I know is getting or has recently gotten a divorce. Why should I think we'll fare any better than Alan Curtis and Joan or John Bauer and Anne? Or any of those people?"

"I don't know why we should fare better," I said, "except that it's us. But look! Don't worry about it. Just come to my house for dinner this Friday night. My mother has invited you. My sisters will be there. My father, of course. You don't have to marry me to have dinner with my family. I had dinner with yours and I don't feel compromised."

"All right," he said, "and you get to keep the car. My half too."

"Oh, that's very generous," I said, and since in those days there wasn't much point in dragging around without a goal in sight, I added, "but now that we'll probably stop seeing each other after Friday night, why don't you keep the car until then and drive it out to Brooklyn when you come for dinner?"

Friday evening when the bell rang, my mother grabbed my arm.

"Shirley," she said, "this is the one. I feel it. I know it. This is the one."

"Please, Momma," I said, "you haven't even seen him yet. Besides, he hasn't asked me. We only bought a car together."

"Asking? What's asking?" she said. "I'm telling you he's the one! Go let him in."

George and my family hit it off right away. He listened to my father's stories and told a few of his own. He called my mother Rose, praised her cooking, and asked for seconds. He even said nice things about the wine—crisp, full-bodied, late-vintage (made the month before in our bathtub).

The fifth week, we didn't see each other. Since my upbringing didn't allow a trial marriage, we had a trial separation.

In the middle of the sixth week he called me up at the office. It was a Wednesday morning.

"Hello," he said. "What are you doing for lunch today?"

"Nothing I can't change," I said. "What do you have in mind?"

"I thought we could get married," he said. "It's my birthday."

"Should I call my mother for a rabbi?"

"No. We'll go down to City Hall."

"Okay. I'll call my mother for a dress. I'd like to be married in a new dress."

I called my mother.

"Momma," I said, "George wants to be married today."

"Married?" said my mother. "You can't get married today. It's Sefirah."

"What's Sefirah?" I said impatiently.

"Sefirah," she said with great calm, "is in the Bible. A commemoration for all those lost during the holocaust when the Jews were escaping from Egypt."

"Yeah, but I can't worry about them now."

"It starts the second night of Passover, which was not quite three weeks ago," she went on, "and lasts for forty-nine days. During that time Jewish people are supposed to abstain from anything joyous. I gather you look on your marriage as a joyous occasion?"

"But, Mother, he doesn't want to wait. He wants to get married today during lunch."

"For people who can't wait," my mother continued as if I hadn't spoken, "there is an intermission. On the thirty-third day of Sefirah, for a few hours, you can get married. I think it's a week from Sunday. I'll call the rabbi."

"Oh, please, Momma, he doesn't want to wait until a week from Sunday. He wants us to go to City Hall today!"

"City Hall?" said my mother, shock in her voice. "They have rabbis in City Hall?"

"No, but he doesn't care about that, Momma. Don't you see, Momma? It's his birthday today!"

"Oh . . . it's his birthday!" said my mother. "Why didn't you say so before?" Blessings on mothers of girls—they're so adaptable. "I'll send Ellenore to your office with your new dress and hat. And the new nightgown and robe we bought. And a little perfume. Lots of Jewish people get married in City Hall. Tell George *mazeltov* and call me after."

In those days there was no waiting for a doctor's permission via certificates of health so we hopped right down to City Hall, where we paid three dollars, filled out a form, and a clerk said a few simple words over us. They were refurbishing City Hall that week and there were men painting the floor all around us but it seemed awfully romantic to me. "I do" when it is said by someone you love has a beautiful sound anywhere.

At that time, in addition to I. J. Fox, I was doing Bab-O

Left: (top) 1934—Standing in awe and admiration behind Hollywood star Claire Windsor at I. J. Fox. (bottom) This was the year of the tonsillectomies. Ellenore, age four (lower left), Lillian, ten (far right), and me, nine (near right of Momma).

Right: (top) 1937—George and I make it to the top of Canada's Hill #69. (middle) 1911—Sister Lillian (left) and me. (bottom) 1929—Me working toward Miss Fulton Street.

1943—As I appeared in book, *Women of Achievement*. The big achievement, I'm eight months pregnant.

1961—Daughter Alix.

1967 — Daughter Laurie.

1904 — Momma and Poppa's wedding picture.

1933 — Husband George the year we were married.

O TV REPORTS, INC.

CLIENT: CLAIROL, INC.
PRODUCT: KINDNESS HAIRSETTER

TITLE: "SHAME ON YOU"

DATE: 12/4/74
LENGTH: 60 SECONDS

RS: Curlers on your

Shame on you.

Curlers in your bed.

Shame on you.

in the store.
on you.

Curlers at the door.
Shame on you.

Curlers, curlers, curlers.
Shame on you.

Kindness - America's Number
One Electric Hairsetter.

RS: Plug it in. Set it
oll 'em up.

Take 'em down.

It's the perfect gift. Kindness Instant Hairsetter from
Clairol.

SINGERS: And it's no more,
no more shame on you.

.V. photoscript of the introductory Kindness commercial. Sold over $25 mil-
on in the two weeks before Christmas . . . and around $70 million the next year.

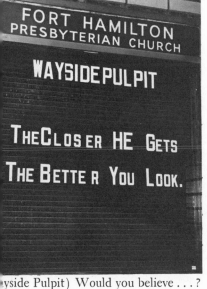

yside Pulpit) Would you believe . . . ?

1967—National Advertising Woman of
the Year.

Every woman should be a redhead   at least once in her life!

New Radiant Red Shampoo-in Hairplor Red by Clairol

Does she...or doesn't she?

Hair color so natural only her hairdresser knows for sure!

MISS CLAIROL HAIR COLOR BATH

If I've only one life,
let me live it as a blo[nde]

Hate
that gray?
Wash
it away!

NEW!
Color only the gray

without changing your natural hair color

Loving Care
Hair Color Lotion by CLAIROL

Why not try
little <u>Loving Care</u> and see!

Is it true...
blondes
have more
fun?

When you dream in color...what color hair do you dream of?
Dreams come truer with Miss Clairol! Does she...or doesn't she?

What does he look at second?

Add a silky new complexion to your legs...as you shave

e gets...the better you look!

RADIO TV REPORTS, INC.

CLIENT: CLAIROL, INC.
PRODUCT: MISS CLAIROL

TITLE: "WYETH"

DATE: 12/4/74
LENGTH: 60 SECONDS

1. SINGER: (VO) She wakes up the sleeping flowers

2. early in the morning,

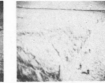

3. early in the morning

4. on her way.

5. Then she lets her hair down

6. when the sun comes up

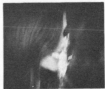

7. then she lets her hair down.

8. ANNCR: (VO) Nothing pretties up a face

9. like a beautiful head of hair ...

10. but even hair born this beautiful

11. needs a little help along the way

12. before gray comes and certainly after.

13. Does she ... or doesn't she?

14. With Miss Clairol Hair-color so natural

15. only her hairdresser knows for sure.

16. Shampoo Formula or Crem Formula.

17. SINGER: And I'll give her my love 'til the day I die.

18. ANNCR: More women use Miss Clairol than any other haircoloring

19. because nature just can't do it alone.

20. SINGER: Yes, I'll give h my love.

T.V. photoscript of a typical Miss Clairol "Does she ..." commercial.

Richard Gelb, president of Bristol-Myers (left), and Bruce Gelb, president of Clairol (right), hear about the forged letter from the "honeymooning blonde" for the first time at the Clairol party.

On each card a slogan. Back of each card, a life time gift.

1973—Arriving at the St. Regis Clairol party with Don Shea, executive V.P. of Clairol (right).

RADIO TV REPORTS, INC.

CLIENT: CLAIROL, INC.
PRODUCT: LOVING CARE

TITLE: "FLOWERS"

DATE: 12/4/74
LENGTH: 60 SECONDS

1. (MUSIC)

2. (MUSIC UNDER) ANNCR: (VO) How long has it been since your husband

3. thought to bring you flowers?

4. Could it be your gray hair makes you seem older than you are?

5. Hate that gray?

6. Wash it away.

7. Wash years away in minutes with Loving Care Hair Color Lotion by Clairol.

8. No mixing. No peroxide.

9. Loving Care pours on right out of the bottle!

10. Colors only the gray.

11. Washes it away without changing your natural hair color.

12. Easy. Used about once a month.

13. Loving Care keeps gray away so you can forget you ever had any.

14. Just choose the tone most like your own.

15. Won't rub off, looks so fresh and natural.

16. Makes your husband feel younger too, just to look at you.

17. So if you hate that gray, wash it away with Loving Care.

18. Not a tint, better than a rinse.

19. Hairdressers agree it's a fountain of youth for graying hair.

20. Loving Care Hair Color Lotion by Clairol.

T.V. photoscript of "soap opera" Loving Care commercial.

Cleanser at Peck Advertising. Bab-O cost two cents more than other scouring powders but we were told it was a little finer in grain so we positioned it as a super-soft scourer, fine enough to use on the finest bathtub enamels in the most luxurious of bathrooms. Sunday supplements then were large newspaper size and the over-all Bab-O format was a full-page halftone keyhole through which one saw a gorgeous towel-draped nude in full color stepping in or out of a beautiful tub. We learned later that these Bab-O ads were favorite pinups in barns all over the country. Detergents that left no ring hadn't been invented yet, so in those days it wasn't ring around the collar but ring around the tub that was the denouement.

Our campaign theme, "A wipe and it's bright!" was meant to assure the housewife that, with Bab-O in the bathroom, she wouldn't have to blow her after-bath cool by scrubbing the tub. My mother had taught us that a nice person, no matter how rich or how many servants she might have, always washed her own tub after she bathed. She said it was a humiliating chore not to be passed on to another person. I never stopped to wonder why she made such a big point about the tub. She didn't seem to feel that way about the toilet bowl. Anyway, that's the way the ads ran and the bathrooms pictured were by courtesy of the luxurious new Waldorf-Astoria. So George and I had access to the manager, who gave us a bargain rate on a double suite for the week since it was the height of the Depression with not too many of them occupied.

That Waldorf suite was magnificent with crystal-drop chandeliers in the living room, two of those gorgeous Bab-O bathrooms, and some of the largest closets I have ever seen. They seemed extra large with my one dress and hat, my one nightgown and housecoat, and just one worn shirt that George had taken off that first night, hanging on a hanger. Washington Square where he lived wasn't too far away so he would always go home to change but it must have been quite confusing to the Waldorf help when they laid out my nightgown in the evening and could find nothing to lay out for the groom. You could tell from the way the drawers were closed and the hangers moved that they did a lot of looking.

We stayed there a week while I gave little lunches for my girl friends dressed in my nice new housecoat. In the meantime, we got a wire from George's father saying that George had "far-feared" me, that is, led me astray. He considered that we were not married at all. There had been no rabbi and, what's more, we had done a wrong thing by being married during the Sefirah.

My mother offered to get the rabbi for that thirty-third-day inter-mission, which was the following Sunday. George thanked her for her co-operation and kindness but said he couldn't accept because he objected on strictly irreligious grounds. Besides, we were leav-ing for the Gaspé Peninsula early that very Sunday morning.

As we were nearing the upper Bronx that next Sunday morning on our way to Canada, George suggested we stop off and visit with a fraternity brother of his. While we were having a drink with Fred and his wife Evelyn, we told them the saga of our marriage. Fred, who knew how George adored his father, put down his drink, went to the phone, called my mother, introduced himself, and asked her to get hold of a rabbi because we were all on our way back to her house for a wedding. We would be there in about three hours—well within the bounds of Sefirah.

It was a Sunday but we managed to find a florist who was open, got him to make up a half dozen gardenia corsages, and sped back to Brooklyn where I found an old cream-colored lace gown in the back of the closet. It looked kind of bridal with the gar-denias so I put it on. By this time my sisters had gathered, the corsages had been distributed, and the rabbi was waiting. That poor rabbi was so flustered by the on-again, off-again quality of the occasion that he kept calling the bride George Halperin and the groom Shirley Polykoff, which made me feel so hilarious I found it impossible to meet my sister's husband's eyes. After the cere-mony was over and we were on our way once again to Canada, we sent a wire to George's father and mother assuring them all was now kosher. George had made an honest woman out of me. That we loved them both very dearly. And that I was now their true daughter in the eyes of all law except Muslims'.

We drove by way of the New England states. It was toward the middle of May and the countryside was fresh and green and there was a beautiful quiet in the air. As we drove along with the top down, we noticed a picturesque little farmhouse with a hand-made sign, "Overnight guests," at the side of the road. It was a lovingly cared-for little house set on a huge tract of neat land. The beds were delicious, the place spotlessly clean, and the price was $1.25 each. This included breakfast. A huge pitcher of fresh orange juice, ham and eggs—I think there must have been eight beautifully fried eggs on that platter surrounded by thick slices of ham. There was homemade jelly and fresh loaves of homemade bread. The two sisters who ran the place were tall and gaunt and straight out of Grant Wood. They obviously needed the money—it was 1933—yet they asked us was there anything else they could give us as we paid our bill of $2.50.

"How do you suppose they manage to make a profit?" I wondered out loud to George as we went back upstairs for our luggage.

"Let's see now," he said. "How do we do this without hurting their feelings?" He took out a five-dollar bill. "What have you got? Something you won't miss."

"What about these bobby pins? Or this comb?" I asked.

"Fine. This looks just fine," he said as he arranged the pins and comb casually over the five-dollar bill. "This way they'll think we forgot it and feel sorry but glad."

We were on our way to the Manoir Richelieu in the Gaspé country and the itinerary included a stop-off at Château Frontenac in Quebec. Forty years ago the Château Frontenac was rated among the top hotels on this continent with specially high marks for its French cuisine. Dinner on the day we arrived was to be our gala wedding celebration and George was determined to make it unforgettable. He did.

While we were still upstairs in our rooms, he phoned the maître d' and asked him to come up for a consultation. Together they planned a magnificent feast. After the first two minutes the maître d', recognizing that he was indeed in the presence of a connoisseur, put away the menus and began to compose a dinner on a special pad with a gold pencil.

I sat there entranced. Spellbound like a Cinderella. A Cinderella from Brooklyn who had somehow won the heart of a true sophisticate, a continental Prince Charming who not only knew what to order but could do it in the original French. The picture of the two conferring over the menu will be forever etched in my mind.

Un menu de gala.

George suggested that we start with a delicate *poisson.* The maître d' put his fingertips to his lips, kissed them, and volunteered *mousseline de saumon* with a *sauce velouté.* (This turned out to be a melt-in-the mouth fluff of fresh poached salmon with a smooth, light lemony sauce. Heavenly.)

"And, of course, with *poisson,*" continued the maître d', "a *vin blanc sec?*"

George said, "*Naturellement.*"

The maître d' said, "Pouilly Fumé '29?"

George said, "*Splendide!* For the main course, a chateaubriand?"

"*Mais oui,*" said the maître d'. "With *sauce Bercy?* Truffles foie gras? Or *simplicité?*"

It was decided on *simplicité* with a good Médoc. Château Margaux. The vegetables, *asperges au beurre.* The salad, a *bouquet des vertes* with a dressing the maître d' would mix himself. And since the dinner would be rather rich, for dessert, *oranges glaceés* touched with a soupçon of orange liqueur.

We had started with Russian caviar and champagne (but what else?) before going down to the dining room and I must say the dinner was exquisite and the wines superb, all served by the maître d' himself while the waiters hovered about rendering homage unto Caesar. I kept right up with George, who seemed complete master of the situation, and when the maître d' suggested we have our coffee and cordials upstairs in the suite, I readily assented.

About five minutes after we reached our rooms, there was a knock on the door and the maître d' wheeled in a huge, well-stocked liquor cart. He set up the table, poured the coffee, set out the glasses, then turned to depart. He bowed to me and then to George. George bowed in return. As the maître d' backed up to the door, he bowed once again to George. George bowed once again to him, this time a little lower. As he was closing the door, the maître d' bowed still again. Not to be outdone, George bowed back but this time he bowed right down to the floor, where he passed out completely.

I was fine. I turned to see whether the liquor cart had turned into a pumpkin but it hadn't, so I drank the coffee and brandy and giggled. I tried to rouse my sleeping prince with a kiss but he wouldn't rouse. After I had checked to make sure he was breathing, I took off his shoes, put a pillow under his head, and went to solitary slumber in the huge king-size bed.

6

Is It True
Blondes Have More Fun?

This may not be fact but it's pretty prevalent fiction. However, rather than stir up a lot of controversy with brunettes and red-heads for whom we were preparing other ideas and products, we decided to leave the question open. Let the consumer figure this one out for herself, we thought. And did she ever!

"I used to run after the bus," wrote one newly made blonde. "Now it stops at my feet."

"Deep inside, I've always known I had a blonde personality," wrote another. "Now I'm letting it all show through. Call me bombshell."

"When I walk down the street, men whistle and call, 'Hey, Blondie.' I turn around to see if it's someone else they mean. But it's me! And I like it, so I won't sign this letter. (signed) Ever grateful."

"Now men don't just pass me by. The other morning I met the milkman unexpectedly and he dropped two bottles of milk."

As you can see, women's consciousness had not as yet expanded to exclude "sex object" as a goal of life.

Every mail brought new assurances. Apparently there were lots of women out there who shared my feelings about being a blonde, which is not altogether surprising when you consider that blonde propaganda traces back thousands of years to the Greek poets, who invented Aphrodite, Diana, and maybe even Helen of Troy, the blonde who launched a thousand ships. (Cleopatra only had a barge.)

"You mean to say," asked my husband incredulously, "that a woman who for fifteen, twenty, or thirty-five years hadn't thought herself desirable could suddenly feel transformed into a bombshell by the mere lightening of her hair?"

I must confess, albeit with a blush, that I answered, "Yes."

It was like something out of a fairy tale, but then, *The Red Fairy Book, The Green Fairy Book, The Blue Fairy Book* were fashionable reading in the days of my childhood. All the princesses who ever let down their hair were blonde. The angel on the Christmas tree was blonde. Most of the expensive sleeping dolls with the big blue eyes were blonde. (We hadn't as yet progressed to Betsy Wetsy.) In those days one had to have a rich aunt who collected expensive foreign dolls while traveling, to discover that dolls could come in different hair colors and complexions. Even in games, the answer to "Knock, knock, who's there?" was "The angel with the golden hair."

In literature, on a higher level, Alexander Pope's Belinda in *The Rape of the Lock* had fair tresses that "draws us with a single hair. . . ." In another rape, but this time of Lucrece by Shakespeare, "Her hair, like golden threads, played with her breath." And W. B. Yeats cheerfully assured Anne Gregory that "only God, my dear, could love you for yourself alone. And not your yellow hair."

In the real world of the twenties, there was Anita Loos, a dynamic little brunette herself, telling the world that Gentlemen Prefer Blondes. A story that's been told again and again on the screen, in the theater, on the late, late movie, and today in song and story by Carol Channing, the original Lorelei herself, in a brand-new Broadway version.

Jean Harlow with her platinum hair and heart of gold, blatantly blonde Mae West inviting him to come up and see her sometime (and he coming, of course). The Gold Diggers of the thirties, the Alice Faye, Lana Turner, June Haver, Betty Grable pinups of the forties and fifties. Not to overlook Grace Kelly, who made it to princess, or that all-time sex goddess, Marilyn Monroe, "I want to be blonde all over."

So in 1957 the time was right, the blonding product was right (a definite improvement on anything that had come before: faster, kinder, softer in tone). And the ad writer must have been right.

I had been brainwashed blonde at birth.

Never having thought of myself as being particularly pretty, I had always felt grateful that I'd at least been born a blonde and that my mother had tried to keep me a blonde. I remember all those lemons she used to squeeze and the camomile tea my head was always being dunked in. To me, this was a special mark of love and attention from my mother. But it's interesting to reflect how every generation has its own standards. When my own daughter, Alix, was seven and her hair began to darken and I tried a lemon rinse on her, she was horrified. "You don't like me the way I am," she said tearfully.

All my mother had to say to make me conform was, "Well, that's how everybody does it." Or "That's the way you do it in America." When I told my second daughter, Laurie, who was five and continually sleeping with her head at the foot of the bed, "Laurie, nobody sleeps with their head at the foot of the bed," she answered, "Well, I do!"

Before getting back to the blondes and while still on my children, let me tell this little story. Our housekeeper, Ernestine, had been promising them colored crayons. For some reason the store she passed on her way in was always out of colored crayons. Finally, in desperation, she bought them a box of white chalk.

"Thank you," said the older politely.

"Oh, I see," said the younger one matter-of-factly, "all different colors of white."

Now let's go back to 1957. It was eight-thirty in the morning and we were in the conference room at Foote, Cone & Belding. There was Rolland Taylor, president of the agency, Leo Rosenberg, account manager, Frank Mayers, newly hired account executive, the art director, Eric Lunden, and me, the writer. We were all nervously tacking up the blonde campaign, a series of about ten ads designed for magazines (television wasn't in the picture much yet) and all the ads of course were built around the joys and advantages of being a blonde.

As I recall the headlines, they read:

1. Is it true blondes have more fun? (Having scored so heavily with the "Does she . . . or doesn't she?" and "Hate that gray?" I was now practically wedded to the arresting question.)
2. Is it true more blondes wear mink?
3. Is it true blondes are never lonesome?
4. Is it true more blondes marry millionaires?
5. Is it true blondes marry younger?

and maybe even, Is it true blondes are never blue? Anyway, there were ten variations on the theme. The presentation was called for eight forty-five in the morning and promptly on the dot the receptionist announced the arrival of the Clairol people, Mr. Lawrence Gelb, president, and Mr. Sheldon Levison, general manager. In those days you dealt directly with top management.

I was terrified at the idea of making a presentation to the head of the company. I thought it would steady my stomach a little if I drank one or two cups of hot water and maybe ate a soda cracker or two. I don't know why I thought that. I'd never tried that remedy before. I gave the order to a mail boy. In the days of the old office buildings, before hot- and cold-water fountains, this was the equivalent of asking for a tall glass of ice water in the middle of the desert. Incidentally, I never saw that mail boy again. But I needn't have worried so much about the meeting. Though Mr. Gelb didn't respond to my campaigns that day, we got to know each other a little better and soon became fast friends. I was fascinated by the unexpected turn of his imagination and grew to admire his intelligence and vision, his dedication and perseverance. It must be pretty wonderful to know you've helped create an industry that has done so much to make a woman feel beautiful.

But that morning, he was less than enthusiastic about the advertising. Discouraged, thoroughly deflated, I mentally put myself back in the closet, which was where most of the copywriters and art directors were kept in the large agencies during the middle fifties.

In those days big agencies were riddled with research and marketing types who specialized in weekly staff meetings of monumental monotony. Meetings that droned on and on with such deadly sameness, they could have been syndicated. Just sign on the bottom line.

And most of the advertising in the fifties reflected this dullness.

Working very closely with research were the account executives. They maintained all the contact with the client and usually had all the say about what went into the ads and what creative efforts were to be shown or not shown. Or, even worse, how an ad should be doctored.

All the account executives were men, of course, regardless of how intimately female the product might be, and quickly raised to vice-president status so that the young brand men at the client could feel they were important enough to merit the attention of a high agency executive. It took what practically amounted to a revolution led by such creative agency heads as Bill Bernbach, David Ogilvy, Fairfax Cone, who were themselves advertising craftsmen of extraordinary talent and ability, to overthrow the system. They not only gave the copywriters and art directors full rein to be creative but allowed them to do the actual selling of their ideas to the client.

This had the obvious advantage of enabling the copywriter to convey her (or his) enthusiasm as well as the complete line of reasoning for the campaign. It could have a hidden disadvantage, however, in that the client might have an ambivalence toward writers because he would have liked to be one himself. Such was the case with Larry Gelb's second son, Bruce. In fact I think he probably would have made a superb copywriter had he not been so busy being vice-president of Clairol and then president, in his turn. Over the twenty years we have worked together, we have hollered, bickered, insulted, outwitted, and destroyed each other regularly, but through it all we always had a mutual professional respect and affection which we used to celebrate periodically by getting extravagantly drunk together, with account man Frank Mayers along to make sure that we didn't do each other in.

At Foote, Cone & Belding, I was particularly lucky with my account men. They had a different attitude toward creative people. Leo Rosenberg was the senior executive, a fatherly type with a wealth of experience. (Which twin has the Toni?, Papermate pens, etc.) He used to walk around reading my copy out loud with just the right inflection. (Could a copywriter ask for anything more?) And Frank Mayers, who at that time seemed awfully young to me, but to whom I immediately felt drawn because of his sensitivity to people and ideas and for his good taste and straight thinking about advertising. Through the years I appreciated even more his quiet persistence that never let me lose a good idea.

We took the blonde ads back to Richard Gelb.

Richard Gelb was Lawrence Gelb's eldest son, who never, as far as we could see, had any problems making decisions about ads or any other matter where his judgment was involved. He assumed that no one would ever have the temerity to present him with anything less than the best. Of course, this was both a burden and a challenge.

He had established himself with us two years previously by buying the "Does she . . . or doesn't she?" campaign for Miss Clairol haircoloring on sight—even before the research proved the impact of the theme. His only stipulation was that we add the words "Hair color so natural" to the line we already had, "Only her hairdresser knows for sure!" The addition of these four little words clarified and sharpened the impact of the ads. Immediately, they were unmistakably haircoloring ads.

That the research results were no surprise to me further confirmed that my thinking reflects the aspirations and anxieties of what is usually called "the average American woman." I find this a very fortunate and important asset in copywriting—if I can't convince myself, then I can't convince anyone else either. In 1955, I had said that if the client was going to spend $19,000 trying to isolate which ten factors were most crucial to a woman considering tinting her hair, the first nine would be some form of "no one should know" and the tenth that it shouldn't harm her hair.

Nine months later the research analysts brought forth their conclusions. The first nine: no one should know; and the tenth: it shouldn't harm her hair.

So now Richard reminded us that he had already approved the idea of the blonde campaign we were recommending some six months before when we had asked that he authorize a test ad featuring the headline in a Los Angeles Sunday supplement.

With some irritation he said, "Why are we still hesitating? Didn't that ad raise sales some three hundred per cent when we ran it in California with just a line drawing? Why shouldn't it do even better nationally with a decent layout and a good photograph?"

It more than did!

We stayed with the one line, "Is is true blondes have more fun?" in print on the theory that the line would take on even larger connotations than haircoloring (as had happened with "Does she . . . or doesn't she?"), and in addition I felt that any woman who was going to take the two and a half to three hours entailed by the process, every three weeks, should have the right to expect something spectacular for her efforts.

We planned the television around vignettes of blondes having a gorgeous time just as we did in the print ads and did a simple tune around a very simple lyric. (In those days, copywriters were still writing their own songs.)

> Is it true blondes have more fun?
> Is it true blondes have more fun?
> A Lady Clairol blonde . . . that's silky, shiny blonde . . .
> A Lady Clairol blonde . . . that's silky, shiny blonde . . .
> Is it true blondes have more fun?

Although, as I have said again and again, what appeals to me appeals to the lady in Dubuque, or Fresno, or Mobile, I was quite surprised to find our advertising appealed also to the lady in the U.S.S.R.

According to the October 1965 issue of *Vogue* magazine, a private wire from Kiev, Russia, had informed them that the newest song hit in the U.S.S.R. was none other than the Clairol television jingle, "Is it true blondes have more fun?"

Isn't it too bad that Clairol had no product distribution in the U.S.S.R. at that time? Who knows? We might have changed the whole political complexion of the country from red to blonde!

Suddenly T.V. comedians, newspaper cartoonists, greeting card manufacturers were capitalizing on the question, "Is it true blondes have more fun?" The publicity was so widespread, I even started getting letters of my own.

Dear Miss Polakoff:

"Only my hairdresser knows for sure whether I am a blonde," you said, on To Tell the Truth television program, several weeks ago. However, I, also, know for sure, and I know that you are a blonde, having met you many years ago, when both of us came to the dental office of Dr. Joseph Goodspeed, Avenue L & Coney Island Ave., Brooklyn.

A few words about the person who would like to have the pleasure of meeting you again. I was engaged in the general practice of law from 1924 to 1935, when I entered the textile business, in which I am still engaged. If I can arrange to make satisfactory transfer of my business to someone, I will plan to again engage in the practice of law, probably in association with some other attorney or attorneys.

If, among the clients of Foote, Cone & Belding, there is some textile firm who would be interested in discussing with me the matter of transfer of my business, I would be glad to have such discussion. I convert pillow-ticking, which I sell to pillow manufacturers; and I manufacture, through a contractor, pillow-ticks, which I sell to stores.

I have never married, and live with my mother, and help to take care of her. Mama, God bless her, is 90 years old, and cannot be left alone. Of course, someone is in the house when I go to business, and when I see friends, etc., etc.

That evening, so many years ago, when I had the great pleasure of enjoying your company, you wore black, and I clearly remember how becoming it was, for this extremely attractive blonde to wear a black dress.

If you care to phone me, best time would be between 1–4:30 P.M. Very often I leave the house late, as I must wait until the woman I employ returns from shopping at grocery, meat store, etc., after having attended to Mama. Thus, very often, I arrive at my office a bit before noon, and then I go out to have lunch.

Cordially
Benjamin ———

Dear Mrs. Pilykolff,

I wont erase mispelling of your name but will merely ask your forgiveness. I must confess I seen your picture in New York Times recently and you look pretty good to me. I am going to suggest that if your not doing anything on 21st between 2:30–3:30 P.M., you come aboard the "Independence" and see me off in Cabin-506 before I embark on this impulsive last minute autumn cruise. I made up my mind yesterday and fortunately got a last minute space. If you do not have the time and regard this as the most unconventional mode, then I will call you upon my return late October or you can take the bull by the horns and try me at 360-8244. Then again if you are an experienced trans-Atlantic voyager you might call me before I leave and give me a few tips on how to behave aboard ship.

Nomadically
J.P. ———

Dear Shirley,

My name is Tony W——— and as you probably guessed I'm a Marine.

I was reading *Time* magazine when I saw this article about you. I find it very hard to put into words but my reason for writing is to tell you that I admire your ambition as a housewife and business woman. I went to school for hairstyling before boredom overtook my thoughts.

If it's at all possible I would like to have a photo of you. And if you would like, I would feel honored to send one of me. I hope that your family don't get upset.

Sincerely yours,
Sir Anthony J.W———

After Thoughts:
Please excuse prints on the letter.

Or the man who, after reading an article on advertising in the *Saturday Evening Post,* began to telephone me at four o'clock every morning. Not to make obscene remarks but to assure me that he would never tell anyone that he was the one who had really written all of my campaigns. When I complained to the telephone company, the supervisor suggested that I put my phone in a drawer at night and cover it with a pillow. When I remonstrated that the remedy seemed a bit primitive in this age of Telstar and other instant international communications, she had another good idea. Why not try reasoning with my midnight caller?

I tried this. "Don't you ever sleep?" I asked him solicitously the next time he phoned. "Why do you have to call so late?"

"Do you think you're the only one on my list?" he answered impatiently. "It takes time to get to you. You're only number nine."

I was hurt. "Number nine?" I said. "Who's number one?"

"Adam Gimbel," he said.

You can imagine that I was quite swept off my feet by such far-flung correspondents. Meanwhile, back at Clairol, the mailman continued delivering small testimonials of bliss.

But at length that company received one letter that stood out from all the rest. It was circulated with covering memos to the Gelbs and to Frank Mayers, Fairfax Cone, Rolland Taylor at Foote, Cone & Belding. (Quote: "Look what we're doing for the ladies!")

The letter, postmarked Bermuda, finally arrived on my desk. It read as follows:

Dear Clairol,

Thank you for changing my life. My boyfriend, Harold and I were keeping company for five years but he never wanted to set a date. This made me very nervous. I am 28 and my mother kept saying, soon it would be too late for me.

I ride the subways every day to work because I am a bookkeeper. Three months ago it was too crowded as usual to get a seat. So I had to stand right in front of your ad which said blondes have more fun.

Harold always looks at blonde girls when they pass by even when I am walking with him, so this started me thinking. I thought maybe I should do something to my own brown hair like your poster says.

That is how I am in Bermuda now on my honeymoon with Harold and writing this letter to thank you for changing my life.

> Best regards
> (Mrs.) Harold ———

A note attached to the above said, "Shirley, is this for real? We are using it as the theme for our national sales meeting. It's almost too good to be true! Moreover, Fax Cone is going to use it as the basis of his speech in Chicago. Any further suggestions?"

I had no further suggestions.

Mrs. Harold ——— received a case of Lady Clairol Hair Lightener in the mail by way of appreciation for all the inspiration she had generated throughout the Clairol Company, for her letter had indeed become the chief testimonial to the power of the emotional approach to advertising.

I know she must have been quite surprised to have that carton delivered to her door since she had (a) not written any letter to us whatsoever, (b) she was, in fact, fifteen years old and (c) was my daughter's best friend in high school. She did have reddish-brown hair and she liked it fine that way, thank you. She remains to this day the least likely candidate for haircoloring I have ever met.

Truth is, I had written that letter and had had it mailed by a friend who'd gone to Bermuda. As a gag, of course. The wording was so earnestly naïve, I had never expected anyone to take it seriously but it had gone so far I didn't know how to back out. Anyway, it was too late. The ploy had exploded beyond any fancy I'd entertained. For six months I lived in terror and could take only a few defensive measures. I called my daughter's friend and told her that if she received a phone call from anyone who wished to discuss either her hair color or her letter, she should say, "You must mean my sister who is honeymooning in Bermuda. She's still away."

The muse who watches over copywriters must have been watching vigilantly over me, for she was never home when they called and they finally gave up.

My forgery remained an important and beloved document through the next eighteen years. It wasn't until my retirement-from-Foote-Cone party given by Clairol in 1973 that I said, "Remember that letter from the girl who got to a Bermuda honeymoon by becoming a blonde?"

There were twenty-two men at the party and every one of them said, "Yes?"

"Well, I wrote it."

After a moment of silent disbelief, the uproarious laughter that welled up all around me made me feel absolved at last.

And speaking about absolution, that same daughter Alix, who had objected to the lemon rinse when she was seven, now, at the age of thirteen and approaching her first formal dance with somewhat shaky confidence, was considering lightening her dark blonde hair on her own.

We had spent a great deal of time selecting her gown, a full-length strapless white tulle to the floor, after the fashion of the fifties, bolstered at top and cinched at the waist underneath by a Merry Widow bra. For those of you who don't remember when a bra was not for burning, the Merry Widow was an engineering marvel that pinched you in the middle and pushed more to the top. But that wasn't enough for Alix. She felt she needed more than just a new dress and a Merry Widow—hence the blonde streaking in her hair.

The night of the dance I thought she looked gorgeous, but she was scared, and I was scared for her.

When she came home that night and into our room, her face had a shy but luminous look. "I was scared," she said, "but as I was walking down the stairs to the ballroom I caught a glimpse of myself in the mirror and I looked so sort of . . . divine."

Now who knows where that confidence was born? She had seen herself in the mirror *before* she left for the dance, but at a certain moment in the evening she suddenly *felt* beautiful. And to *feel* beautiful is the real key. This is true at any age.

Anyway, my daughter subsequently became quite social and popular with her peer group, as they say. For a while she was almost convinced that the blonde streaks did it. I hadn't meant to be quite that convincing, so to preserve my own sanity and the sanity of parents in general, our T.V. commercials for the blonde lighteners carried the line, "Chances are she'd have gotten that young man anyhow . . . but you'll never convince her of that!"

Recognition of the importance of *feeling* beautiful led us to the second campaign on blondes, the campaign for the older woman, thirty-five and up (the first having been oriented to those under thirty-five). This second campaign was also a logical consequence of the first, for if it's true that blondes have more fun, then "If I've only one life, let me live it as a blonde!" is an obvious conclusion.

So fast did this catch on that one man wrote us a letter saying his children were growing up to believe hair didn't gray with age, it just turned blonde.

In a Sunday broadcast on radio station WBAI in March 1966, Rollo May, the existentialist philosopher, singled out the line "If I've only one life, let me live it as a blonde!" as the "ultimate existential statement."

Of course this thinking was also adaptable to redheads and brunettes, for the core of the message for everyone was "Live it!"

So for the redhead products we wrote, "Every woman should be a redhead at least once in her life!" This T.V. commercial won the first prize at the International Film Festival in Venice, 1968. And for the younger teen-age blondes we wrote, "Just enough lightening to stir up a storm." For brunettes, "You can be a rich brunette (the kind men marry)" and for all colors, "Beautiful hair, a man could get lost in it."

However, it was already increasingly evident that the prescription "Live it!" was more easily lived by one half of the population than another—and I don't mean blondes rather than brunettes. I mean men as opposed to women. As I said before, in the fifties copywriters were kept in the closet and rarely (if ever) promoted to vice-presidencies, but if you were both a copywriter and a woman, that was double jeopardy.

I remember in 1958 the New York *Times* decided to do a success story on the "Does she . . . or doesn't she?" campaign featuring the copywriter. The Clairol Company called Mr. Taylor to represent the ad agency in the interview. Not being the writer, Mr. Taylor declined with thanks and suggested that I, the writer, go instead. Clairol, who at that time had no women in the management hierarchy or in the product groups, thought it was unseemly for a woman to be the focus of the story. But the New York *Times* decided to kill it rather than run it without interviewing the writer. No writer, no article.

I love you, New York *Times*.

Reluctant to lose the publicity, Clairol finally gave the go-ahead and this first article became a milestone in my career. It triggered all kinds of write-ups and television appearances for the next fifteen years.

Nonetheless, this sort of publicity was, at that period of my life, a two-edged sword. At the same time that I was wrestling for recognition and status at the office, I was trying to keep my career within manageable bounds at home, at least as far as my salary was concerned, so as not to threaten my husband's psyche. The legal profession didn't pay as highly as advertising in those days and I did not want my salary to rise above $25,000, which was what he made. But I did yearn to be a vice-president, which accounted for the impasse; they wanted to give me money while keeping me behind the scenes and I wanted to be a vice-president and recognized as such.

The other concession I made to my marriage was born of my own fear and was not a response to anything my husband demanded of me because he was as liberated for the time as any man I've ever known. This concerns the use of two separate names. I was Shirley Polykoff in the office, having already established a reputation under my maiden name, and Polly (a fore-shortening of Polykoff) Halperin at home. I did this for two reasons. First of all, I didn't want anyone ever to call *him* Mr. Polykoff, but most of all, I was apprehensive about straining his good will toward career women by having my office identity overwhelm my identity as his wife.

Today, I think the movement in some feminist circles to have the woman maintain her maiden name even in marriage has several definite advantages, the chief of which is that she doesn't have to feel apologetic if her professional identity continues after 5 P.M.

In my case, so separate was Shirley Polykoff from Polly Halperin that many people didn't know the two were, in fact, one.

This schism was particularly difficult to maintain because, as I have noted before, advertising demands that the copywriter be completely immersed in the product. Often I would lie awake at night going over some three or four words for hours, trying to fit the essential selling point into just the right cadence.

The obsession with the nuances of a product can be carried to heights rarely dreamed of by the consumer when she (or he) reads the final copy. For example, let us take the Mustang story, which I was once asked to relate to a national advertising conference, although I myself neither wrote the campaign nor worked for J. Walter Thompson, the agency that produced it for Ford. The representative from J. Walter Thompson was handling another section of the conference at the same time and because we could draw a parallel between the emotional approach of the Mustang commercials and the Miss Clairol commercials I was elected to give the Ford story.

Now naming a new product, whether it's a car, a cosmetic, or a food, plays a key role in how or where the product will be positioned in the market. So important are these preliminaries that most agencies have a special group composed of creative people to handle it. At that time J. Walter Thompson had what they called the Forward Planning Group to take over these essentials. This group literally lived at Ford in the early months of the car's development. And like everyone involved in the introduction of anything new in an agency, the Forward Planning Group worked under the tightest security. This one worked in a long, narrow, windowless room which a member of the group had christened the Tomb (you see, everything needs a name to have an identity). Only three J. Walter Thompson people had a key to the Tomb. The office cleaning women had none. All the tidying up was done by building guards. Even the wastepaper was burned under the watchful eyes of the Forward Planners (intimations of Watergate?).

Stashed away in the Tomb, the creative team, both copy and art, were very much involved with three vital elements: (1) positioning the car; (2) naming the car; and (3) finding a way to convey the excitement of its personality to everyone concerned with launching it, as well as to the consumer.

What was so great about this particular car? Every year Detroit goes slightly mad with the new season's entries. And sometimes the new season's entries don't seem too different from the old season's entries. So you can imagine what kind of mental gymnastics the copywriters have to go through. But there was something in the look of this new car that set it apart. Its silhouette generated excitement. The hood was stretched out and the trunk compartment shrunk. (Introducing the car with a shrunk trunk?)

The car had what they called a mouthy front end. (Introducing the car with the motor mouth?)

However, the low-slung, long-hooded look would take it out of the compact class into the sports car field. That was okay because the peppy engine, the four-speed stick shift, the bucket seats seemed to put it right into the fancy Italian racer class, new features bound to make a hit with the younger element.

But Daddy pays for the car and he's got other members of the family to consider besides his sporting elder son, so the car was going to have to hold onto this racy look without loss of family comfort and practicality. So now we're looking for a name that will characterize this proud-spirited, Italian, all-purpose-family-racing-car hitherto known only as number T-5.

The choice was narrowed to five hundred names. And from that list came a name reflecting current public interest in things Italian. And since the car did reflect some of the features of the Italian racing cars in the Torino auto show, it was natural that a name like Torino should become the leading favorite.

Now the time had come to start the wheels turning, to put the car in its proper environment on the highway as people would see it. And that called for an actual car so it could be filmed and shown around to top management to prove they really had something in this new car. (I've often wondered why one has to interest top management in the value of one of its own products.)

But Ford had only this one hand-made operating model that in truth didn't operate too well. By now they'd spent nearly $200,-000 but the car still had no shock absorbers. The doors didn't work. The car had been driven only by engineers who must have been over six feet tall because the front seats were bolted down in far back position to accommodate only drivers over six feet tall or shorter drivers who could drive while lying down, with their toes stretched out.

Finally all this was taken care of and the car was delivered under wraps in a closed van to Ford's extensive proving grounds, about thirty-five miles from Detroit. And now the boys and girls really went to work. Twenty-five J. Walter Thompson people—artists, writers, photographers, television experts—met that van and worked for three days and into the nights not only on moving pictures and stills but on ideas. Ideas being the most difficult commodity of all to come by.

Finally there emerged a film of the car driving through a field of corn, literally, and coming to a halt. The doors opened and out stepped two people in evening clothes. He with a smart straw picnic basket. She in a long slinky black gown and carrying—what else?—a lighted candelabrum. (Nothing so appropriate as candelabra in the cornfield.) The car itself, Torino, "a brand new import—from Detroit," priced at a modest $2,368 F.O.B. Detroit.

"F.O.B.?" you ask. Free on Board. In Detroit. Every place else gets a freight charge and how many of us live in Detroit?

Anyway, everybody who saw the car guessed it to be much, much higher in price. So suddenly the whole thing seemed very American instead of Italian. Very American efficiency. Which meant the subject of names had to be reopened and Torino was dropped in favor of the all-American horse. Mustang was suddenly discovered to have scored even better than Torino.

The copy was revised to read, "The Mustang has the look, the fire, the flavor of the great European road cars, yet it is as American as its name! And its name is Mustang." After all that travail. Torino found its own place in the sun a few years later but probably not without an equally long and agonizing scenario.

And that is how I know that, whether one writes for cars, cleansers, or cosmetics, every copywriter has to be a little bit crazy.

7

The Closer He Gets
the Better You Look

It was 1964. I had been a widow for three years and still had not wholly reconciled myself to the new status. If you've had a good marriage, and ours had lasted twenty-seven years, it's pretty hard to carry on alone or start a whole new pattern of living. Not that a life together for two strong characters is all that smooth or that I didn't have plenty of time to prepare for it. George's death was slow and cruel but he bore it with dignity. It was as if he'd lived his whole life to die with dignity—once he learned that there was no cure for what he had. It was I who told him.

He'd been operated on in 1958 and the doctors told only me that they'd found cancer in the stomach. They were sure they'd gotten it all out and thought it wisest not to tell him. I agreed. In later years, it seemed ironic to me that a man who used to wake up shaking in the middle of the night to tell me he had just had or was about to have a heart attack was to linger on for two more years until he became so emaciated he looked like a Dachau case because his heart just wouldn't give up.

But at that time he appeared to be recovering rapidly and we went off to Europe as we had planned. I kept the secret of the cancer to myself. In fact I think I believed, as the doctor had assured me, that we had it licked. So I tried not to think about it, consciously anyway, though at times, when we were getting about in Venice or walking along the streets of Rome or Paris, I'd burst out crying. At the moment I didn't know why I was crying but suddenly everything looked so sadly beautiful.

We had been home about a year when there was a recurrence of pain, but greater, much greater pain than anything George had experienced before. Again there were painful examinations with torturing enemas and X rays and finally a private consultation between the doctor and me.

"Liver," he said. "We have no way." He tried to cheer me, "But what we did on the stomach is fine."

"Oh, great!" I thought. And then, "How long, Doctor?"

"Six months," he said. "Maybe."

It was during this phase, when he didn't know and I had not yet accepted the diagnosis, that I ran around trying to track down every rumor and news story about someone incurable being cured by some miracle formula or some doctor proclaiming a radical breakthrough. There was nothing. Yet for the next few weeks the doctor continued to schedule X rays and before each X ray George had to subject himself to painful and exhausting enemas.

I called the doctor. "Doctor, I thought you said there was no hope."

"There is no hope."

"Then why are you torturing my husband?"

"We try to keep up appearances," he said. "We think it's better."

But I didn't agree. One day when George was preparing for still another X ray I saw the agony on his face and I said, "George, don't do it. Don't take the enema."

He said, "Why? Maybe this time they'll find something."

"They already have."

"Can't they do anything?"

"There's nothing to do. I've been all over and there's nothing to do."

He walked out of the room. When he came back he looked different. "One out of four," he said. "I'm glad I'm the statistic in this family."

From that time on we never discussed the imminence of his

death. Every morning he'd dress and go to the office, refusing to take his pain pills despite his suffering because he wished to remain lucid enough to arrange his affairs at the office and to keep up the front at home. Since that was the way he wanted it, the girls and I respected his need to avoid openly acknowledging the terrible truth. This had two effects: on the one hand, it prevented us from offering the solace we longed to extend, but on the other hand, it enabled us in the final days to endure with seeming equanimity his wasting away to an almost unrecognizably gaunt stranger.

Years before, George and I had promised each other that in the event one of us contracted an incurable sickness, the other would see that enough pills were available for a quick and certain demise. Keenly aware of his suffering, I marveled that George never took advantage of the pills I always made sure were within easy reach; even those last three weeks at the hospital when there was surely no hope for him. I could only conclude that, when the future no longer exists and the dying are left with nothing more than the immediate present, concerns contract: larger issues such as the quality of life or the right to choose a shorter, less humiliating death are replaced by worrying whether the plants will consume too much oxygen if left in the hospital room overnight.

Mercifully for him, after the first week he had longer and longer periods of unconsciousness but for us, watching the gradual erosion of a human being we loved, there was no surcease.

"Doctor," I begged, "why don't you let him go?"

"I only promised you he would have no pain."

So we kept vigil by the bed, praying each day would be his last, and that's a very strange dilemma to which modern medicine has delivered us: you have to pray for the death of someone you fervently wish were not dying.

There were two lucid moments in the last days. One in which George expressed hope that he would still be here on his next birthday (he was to have been fifty-seven on May 10 some six days hence, which was also our wedding anniversary.) The other was to say, "I can't thank you enough for my life."

He died on May 6 and because he had wished it I postponed his burial until the tenth—although it was against the Orthodox credo not to bury the dead the following day. For months after his death the girls and I had to look at old pictures of George when he was well in order to drive out the image of George when he was dying.

That first year was very difficult in many ways. Aside from my mourning, I found out that many friends who had considered me an individual in my own right when I had a husband now considered me only half a couple, a painful reminder of the half who was no longer present, and still another extra woman to be cared for at a dinner party. I realized I had to make a whole new circle of friends who hadn't known George and me together—an effort I didn't feel up to at the time.

Laurie, who had decided not to go to college out of town so that I wouldn't be alone that first year (my older daughter Alix was married and living on the West Coast), observed one evening that living with me had become like living in a morgue, no people, no music, no color, no fun. With her characteristic straightforwardness she had come to the heart of the matter. I had to find a new way to be.

I redid the apartment, started having people in to dinner, and took up a whole new group of art-oriented pursuits (it was a field I had always neglected in favor of literature and writing), and I encouraged Laurie to apply to a school away from home. I joined the museums, read art books, went to the galleries, bought pictures, even started a project of my own, a wool needlepoint rug with an abstract design created by Sally Kaplan, a friend of mine who is a fine artist. This rug was my late, late night companion during the next few years. Whenever I couldn't sleep, out came the rug. I'd do two lines, stare into the design, and sink into a reverie. It was the only time I allowed myself to think about George.

I remembered the time we went to a wake for the mother of an Irish Catholic friend of ours. I did not go up to the open coffin because I had never seen death and was afraid. But George did. He knelt at the casket and seemed to be saying a prayer, which struck me as odd since he knew nothing of the Catholic liturgy.

"What were you doing, George?" I asked. "Saying a prayer?"

He nodded. "In Hebrew. Just in case God doesn't understand Latin."

Or I'd find myself thinking about George's mania for punctuality, about getting places on time, about making trains and planes.

He would keep reminding me nervously again and again about the hours and the minutes that were passing and of his certainty that we were going to be late no matter where we had to go. Irascibility at such times was really a characteristic of his, and his tremendous decency, integrity, and generosity were in conflict with his very low threshold of impatience. I, on the other hand, hated any strain in the atmosphere. To avoid this kind of nagging, as I called it, I had trained myself to dress as fast as he did, provided he shaved. But that didn't seem to make much difference. And finally I'd had it up to here. "Listen, George," I said, "I'm tired of Chamberlain-ing around." Chamberlain-ing as in Chamberlain, the Englishman with the umbrella who traveled across the English Channel on his knees to appease Mr. Hitler. "If I'm going to get the lecture anyway, though I don't recall when I've ever missed a plane, I might as well take my time. So what if I'm late? I get the nagging either way!"

"Okay. Okay," he said. "Why should I be the policeman? From now on, I promise you, I shall never again mention time, no matter how late I can see you're going to be."

That next week we had an eight-thirty theater curtain. He must have tried nobly because up to seven-thirty he hadn't said anything about our getting ready on time. We'd already had our dinner and were only ten minutes away from the theater, so there really was no need to rush. Suddenly I heard his voice from the other room. "Hey, Poll," he called cheerfully, "notice how I'm not saying we're going to be late!" Ten minutes later, "Hey, Poll," a little less cheerful, "notice how I'm not saying it's twenty of eight?" And from then on, for the rest of his life, it was exactly how it had been before, just prefixed with the words, "Notice how I'm not saying . . ."

Another one of his foibles I remembered was the observance of Mother's Day and its commercialism. "No one has to tell me when to buy my mother or children's mother a present!" he used to say. "I buy a gift when the spirit moves me." And he did. He used to bring home those long-stemmed red roses or a beautiful bottle of wine, unexpectedly and often.

As it happens, I too objected to the commercialism of Mother's Day but I couldn't bear the thought of not getting a present when other mothers did. So we conpromised, as my mother used to say. He observed only four days for me: Christmas, birthday, anniversary, and Mother's Day. The other three hundred and sixty-one days he was on his own to gift as the spirit moved him. But never, never was he ever to bring a gift as a peace offering or to make up for a hurt. That was an attempt to bribe and not allowed.

We had a very good arrangement about fights, I think. We didn't believe like the hero in Eric Segal's *Love Story* that "love means never having to say you're sorry." We believed quite the opposite. We believed that the one who was right in a fight had to apologize. You can see how nicely that could work out. When the one who's right says, "I'm awfully sorry, honey, I was so wrong about so-and-so" or "I really didn't mean to so-and-so," the one who was wrong is so melted down by the magnanimity of the other that it becomes a beautiful reconciliation.

When I was first married to George, I didn't mind it at a picture show when people around me talked. But when you live with someone for a while you get to know the little things that bother him and you try to spare him, not only to keep him happy but because it makes your own life more pleasant too. George couldn't stand it if anyone talked anywhere near him in the theater or the movies. So we stayed away from family-type places. But one time when there was a picture playing at the Radio City Music Hall, we decided to chance it. It was a picture built around a court scene and he was very anxious to catch all of the dialogue. As luck would have it, the first two empty seats together were next to two women who obviously hadn't seen each other for some time and had come to the movie to visit. As soon as our eyes became accustomed to the light we noticed two other seats several rows in front. We got up and took them. The movie was just getting into the court scene when the man next to George started explaining the action to his lady friend.

George nudged his neighbor. "Would you mind speaking a little louder? I can't hear you." He pointed to the screen. "The actors are making too much noise."

The man looked at George for a moment as if he were crazy. "Wise guy!" he said but he did stop talking. However, it was a bad night. The row in back of us was occupied by what must have been a theater party composed of people who weren't fascinated by court scenes because suddenly there was a lot of conversation going on. Noticing the irritation on my husband's face, I turned around and said, "Sssshhh!" It didn't stop the conversation so I turned around and said, "Sssshhhh!" again. The man who was talking paused long enough to say, "Aw! Go hire a hall!" George started to rise. "Come on, let's get out of here." But I wasn't willing to change seats again. I pulled him back to his chair. "Take it easy, Dutch," I said in a stage whisper, "put that gun away." The gangster Dutch Schultz was still very much at large and wanted by the police. Suddenly we were surrounded by an island of peace. It turned out to be a great picture.

There were other public nuisances that George didn't approve of like ladies in curlers at the supermarket, on the street, or in busses. So prevalent was this practice that one wondered when, if ever, the actual hair-do went on view. In later years, when Clairol marketed the Kindness electrically heated Instant Hair Curlers, it was an attempt to solve this problem. Now there would be no need to spend more than seven to ten minutes on this tedious task. Counting on the fact that most men probably felt the same way George had, I did a campaign designed to make women aware of this feeling. A full photoscript of this appears in the photo insert.

> Curlers in your head . . . shame on you!
> Curlers in your bed . . . shame on you!
> Curlers at the door . . . shame on you!
> Curlers in the store . . . shame on you!
> Curlers, curlers, curlers . . . shame on you!

This one commercial really struck a sympathetic chord. It brought sales of 25 million the first year, 70 million the second, and for several Christmases made Kindness Instant Hair Curlers the gift most purchased by men of all ages for the women in their lives, which should give you an idea of how they felt about the old all-day curlers to begin with.

This popularity for the Instant Hair Curlers continued until the advent of long straight hair made any curlers obsolete. Today, however, with the return of the shorter curly look, they should be coming back into use again. Advertising and products that succeed reflect trends in fashion as well as inaugurate them and are great indications of the tempo of the times, which is why it's so much fun to look at old ads and why the current vogue for the twenties and thirties seems almost fresh today.

Recently, we did a new series of Miss Clairol ads reproducing in one corner the original photograph and ad of a mother and child that ran some fifteen years ago, and contrasted it with a larger photograph of the same model as she appears today. The old ad includes the original "Does she . . . or doesn't she?" "She still does!" headlines the updated photograph. How reassuring this should be to women concerned about the long-range effects of using haircoloring. What forceful evidence of the original promise to keep the hair in splendid condition. We were amused to see that even those first ads from the late fifties and early sixties hardly seem dated, which shows how enduring and endearing is the concept of the clean and wholesome girl (now woman) who lives next door.

George used to say, "You must bear with my impatience about small matters. You'll find me a tower of calm about the big things."

When I complained that my life was just a matter of small matters and that I had to take the big calm on trust, he'd pat me on the head and say, "Well, you've been lucky so far, but you'll see whenever the time comes." And I did. We needed a lamp for Laurie's room.

He said, "I guess you can pick one up at Bloomingdale's."

I said, "Please come with me. I'm the only wife I know who has to shop alone. I'm the only wife I know who has to hang up her own pictures. I'm the only wife I know who has to sandpaper the paint off a secondhand piece of furniture herself."

George said, "I don't like to sandpaper old furniture. I'm not good with a hammer and nails. I'm a lawyer."

"That doesn't mean you can't come buy a lamp with me. For your own daughter's room. And let's take the car too," I said, "like other people do."

"It's Saturday," said George patiently. "There's no place to park near Bloomingdale's. There's no place to park anywhere near Lexington and Fifty-ninth Street."

"I'll find you a place," I said.

We took the car and after circling around Bloomingdale's several times I sighted a spot.

He said, "It's too near the hydrant. We'll get a ticket. That's twenty-five dollars."

I said, "Oh, come on, there's plenty of space. You're so legal."

"Okay," he said, "I bow to your superior judgment."

We could find no lamp that suited us both in Bloomingdale's. "Let's drive down to Eighth Street. Right off Greenwich Village," I said. "There are lots of stores around there with lamps. See the value of bringing the car?"

When we got out to where we'd left the car, there was a police ticket for illegal parking on the windshield. Without a word he took the ticket, folded it up, and put it in his pocket. We drove down to Eighth Street in stony silence.

The man in the store said, "We have just this one lamp up here." He pointed to a large pottery base at the head of the stairs. It was a little large but I liked it well enough. I reached out to turn its light on. I was still feeling shaky from the police ticket incident and I must have hit it wrong. The lamp swung out over the stair well on its cord, hit the opposite wall without breaking, then came back to its base in slow motion and smashed to pieces. I wanted to die. The storekeeper said, "That will cost you twenty-seven fifty for the base. That's wholesale."

Twenty-seven fifty plus twenty-five for the ticket and still no lamp! I started to cry. George paid the man. "The hell with lamps," he said, presenting me with his pocket handkerchief. "Let's get a drink."

Because George was not an easygoing, one-of-the-fellers kind of guy, he did not participate in the weekly "boys' night out" of his friends and colleagues. However, he did feel wistful about their camaraderie, even though he didn't like to play cards and thought that macho bar-hopping was a waste of time and money. One man in particular, however, used to incite his reluctant envy. That was Arthur, a lawyer friend of ours. "That Arthur," he used to say, "I have to give him credit. He's really a man about town."

One morning, as we were dressing, he said it again. This was beginning to build. "Look, George," I said, "why don't you take, er, you'll pardon the expression, the night off? It's Thursday. The nurse'll be out. I'd love to have the kids and the kitchen to myself for a change."

"That's sweet of you," he said. "I think I just might try it."

That night he came home at a quarter of one.

"Good! You're still up," he said. "I had a marvelous evening." He unwrapped a large white napkin. "Here, taste this cake." He grinned. "I made it myself."

I followed him into the kitchen. "What do you mean, you made it yourself? With flour and eggs and all that sort of thing?"

"Well, let's say I helped make it."

"Where under the sun . . ."

"I dropped up at Arthur and Lasty's. Arthur was out of course, but Lasty was there and her sister, Portland. Fred Allen's wife. What a struggle when she first married Fred. Comedians didn't make any money at all in those days. But she was used to hard luck! Seems their father was an itinerant medicine man. We practically had each other crying as to who was poorer when we were kids."

"And here I had you doing the night clubs. The Twenty-one or at least El Morocco!"

"We baked the cake while I waited around for Arthur," he continued, "but he never showed. That Arthur." He shook his head admiringly. "He really is a man about town."

"Guess where Arthur was," I said.

"Where? Where?" he asked excitedly.

"Here," I said quietly. "All evening. Know what he said when he left?"

"I give up."

" 'That George,' he said, 'he sure is a man about town.' "

As I stitched away on the rug, making snail's progress, I'd go over things that happened when the kids were small. I was fortunate enough in those days to make sufficient money to have both a housekeeper and a full-time children's nurse to turn to in case of emergency.

While I had the luxury of knowing that my children were not out roaming the halls of the apartment building unattended or wandering around in the streets, I never had peace of mind no matter how high-priced the foreign-trained nannies were. With one exception, they tended to be arrogant, grudging, and condescending toward me and overauthoritarian with the children. Each one came complete with her own set of eccentricities and it often took months to discover that their shortcomings outnumbered their capabilities in the nursery.

I remembered one Miss Schultz, who evidently got undue pleasure from her bowel movements, a sybaritic satisfaction I found out about by coming home unexpectedly one afternoon and hearing wails of ecstasy issuing from the bathroom. Or Miss Johnson, who was most fascinated by my eldest daughter's not yet budding breasts, for she delighted in decorating them with peaks of foam in the bubble bath. This sport might not in itself be a telling one, but when combined with the fact that she used to beat the hands of my youngest daughter, if they strayed beneath the blanket, added up to something less than the ideal mother substitute.

I don't think it was just ill luck on my part to employ a disproportionate share of these frustrated ladies. On Thursdays, my nurse's day off, I would sit in Washington Square Park on the green bench with a phalanx of other nannies and hear them eagerly vie with one another over who had outwitted her employer most cunningly. (The employer was always referred to as "She.") One especially harrowing tale involved a nanny explaining her friend's technique of turning on the gas just enough to help her charges fall asleep as soon as "She" went out for the evening.

I guess my favorite recollection along these lines were of Nurse Dorita. "Dorita Douche Bag," we used to call her because when George and I came home after a weekend away, from every closet we opened up the next few days—the linen closet, the hall closet, the laundry closet, the kids' closet—there tumbled out an inexplicable rainbow of douche bags; pink douche bags, green douche bags, coral, beige, white douche bags. There must have been more than a dozen. We sent her packing, douche bags and all, but they continued to pop out of closets unexpectedly from time to time.

I felt guilty about each new woman I hired and paralyzed after each one was in turn fired.

In those days a "career woman" who also had a family to

care for was regarded so skeptically at the office that, although you could call in and say, "I'll be out this morning to go to the dentist or doctor," you couldn't call in with the excuse that you had to stay home with the children because there was no one to leave them with.

I felt as though I were damned if I did and damned if I didn't. If I had a governess at home, I had to worry about what she was doing or not doing in my absence, and if I didn't have a governess, I couldn't go to my job.

For these reasons, I am today an earnest advocate of universal day care centers with qualified and conscientious personnel so that all women who want to work can have the peace of mind of knowing their children are being cared for in an interesting and empathetic environment.

It's true that trained governesses are no longer available or affordable to working mothers now, but as I have indicated I don't think the old system was any good anyway because inevitably those women resented their status as surrogate mothers and wished themselves, for both power and prestige, to be *the* lady of the house.

In those days, day care centers had not been recognized as a legitimate demand of the nation's working mothers because the women's movement had not yet constructed its modern platform.

In the pre-lib world of advertising too, the Freudian principle that sex was the main motivation for a person's actions had not as yet been challenged, and therefore a number of research organizations came into being that proposed to measure for the client the sex appeal of any ad and suggest ways the agency could intensify it. Vital signs they measured in a test audience were eyeball flutter, fingertip tingle, palm-of-the-hand perspiration, as well as how many people in the audience had changed their minds positively as the result of one single exposure to a television ad. A large number of commercials, some of which are still running and others you may recall, originated in a climate that stressed the "hidden phallic magnetism" of the client's product and packaging.

Thus were born Ajax's white knight, Mr. Clean, the white tornado in the kitchen, Big Wally, the tattoo on the Marlboro man, and Clairol's campaign for a woman's cosmetic shaving cream for legs, "What does he look at second?"

We called this "psyching the commercials" or "putting them on the couch" and even called in a practicing psychoanalyst to verify our own lay insights. Our session was to begin at lunch in a private executive dining room on the fifty-sixth floor of the Pan American Building. There were to be just four of us! the doctor-analyst and Frank Mayers, by that time the account supervisor at Foote, Cone & Belding, Chuck Palmer, the marketing director of Clairol, and I. I came early and sought to set the scene by pulling up the blinds to reveal the stunning splendor of the city stretched out below. This was the kind of meeting room movies are made of—formal Federal furniture, highly waxed and buffed, thick wall to wall carpeting, and a long, brilliantly polished oval table, complete with double candelabrum. (Ah, the candelabrum again.)

When the others arrived I offered the analyst the best seat in the house, the one closest to the windows, commanding the widest view. His manner seemed distracted and his face pale but I thought maybe he was uncomfortable so far from his office consultation couch.

Oddly, he remained standing with his back to the scenery and after a minute of silence he exploded for the door. "I can't stand heights," he said with barely controlled hysteria. "Isn't there some place we can do this on the ground floor? Or," he pleaded, "get those blinds down, please." Which we did, plunging the room into twilight. After placing his seat so it faced the blank inner wall and a round of drinks, for purely medicinal purposes, he regained his composure and the session got under way.

After a review of some of the photoscripts of commercials we had done, he applauded two, in particular, for their libidinal connotations. The Loving Care Hair Color Lotion (see Chapter 4) for its line, "Makes your husband feel younger too, just to look at you," and its accompanying visual of a fountain of water shooting up into the air, and the one we were currently working on for the cosmetic shaving cream for legs. For this latter campaign, we had dug into the past and, remembering the many bull sessions at school when we girls never could agree on what "he" looked at first, I had come up with the line, "What does he look at second?" See print ad in the photo insert.

So the commercial opened with "What does he look at second?"

while we saw a girl walking on the beach wearing a man's black turtle-neck sweater, exposing her lovely long smooth legs. As the announcer followed with "Girls! Add a silky new complexion to your legs . . . as you shave!" the beach scene dissolved to the girl's own bathroom. Here, over the selling copy, we saw her seated shaving her legs. To trigger off an even more sensual response in the viewer, the analyst prescribed a masterful touch: both legs must rise slowly in the air as the girl leaned back in her chair (a position normally associated with an activity other than shaving). Then the scene dissolved back to the girl walking on the beach.

After the addition mentioned above, the commercial was researched and came up with an extraordinarily high persuasion number and a very low interest curve. After puzzling over how you could persuade a woman without interesting her, we went ahead on the basis of the persuasion number. However, we should have paid more attention to the interest curve because, in the actual market, the product bombed dismally. It turned out no woman at that time, rising legs notwithstanding, was interested in paying for a shaving cream when she could use her husband's or a bar of soap that was readily at hand.

Which brings me back to a night in '64 when I was getting to the end of the rug and trying to psych out the territory for a new Clairol haircoloring product I had just been given at Foote, Cone & Belding—a haircoloring that was sloshed on all over the head like a shampoo instead of being applied strand by strand to the new hair only.

Previously, when the longer hair had received more color applications than the new growth nearer the scalp, this type of product produced a horizontal striped effect. That the problem was solved and that beautiful, even, natural-looking color was now a cinch to achieve with a shampoo would have to be the message in the advertising.

As I stared at the rug design, my mind wandered back to those early days when George and I used to meet each other after work and I'd spend the afternoon anticipating the rush of joy when I'd first glimpse him coming down the block. We'd be flying toward each other but, compared to our eagerness to bridge the distance, it was like wading through molasses. Though the street was crowded, we were alone, the people in our path merely obstacles to cut around. On about the fourth time we met this way, he lifted me off my feet with a hug of sheer happiness. We were both a little breathless and as we stood there grinning at each other he said, "You know, you look pretty good from far."

"And from near?"

"Even better."

As I sat there recalling those delicious days, the campaign for Nice 'N Easy shampoo-in hair color unfolded like a dream. And, as if in a dream, the man and woman in the commercial would float toward each other in slow motion across the fields or through the crowds with arms outstretched in anticipation. Though the message would have to express to the consumer that the color results would be even enough to pass closest inspection, it would also have to capture the romance of the visual. And that is how I hit on the line, "The closer he gets the better you look!" "With Nice 'N Easy, it's hair color so natural, the closer he gets the better you look." See print ad in the photo insert.

This campaign had a long active life and fostered a rash of take-offs on T.V., in full-length movies, and in the commercials of other companies. And thus Clairol Nice 'N Easy became the biggest personal-care introduction of its time.

8

To Know You're the Best You Can Be

Winding up a book like this is a little like winding up one's career or even one's life. And telling it all—the way it was—is like lying on a psychiatrist's couch with the readers as my analyst. Much has been written about the problems of retirement, about the psychological stresses that develop *after* a person who has been active and involved all his life suddenly faces interminable, routineless days and years with nothing to do, with no deadlines to meet, no challenges to engage the mind. Or body either, unless it's to cut down on his or her golf handicap.

Perhaps more should be said about the *before* part. More should be said about what happens to a healthy, active person like me, unwillingly faced with compulsory retirement—especially if the years just preceding have been the most successful and productive of the entire career.

Watching the subtle and not so subtle preparations that began getting under way about three years before my actual doom's date couldn't have been too different from sitting in on preparations for my own demise. Or more depressing.

In advertising agencies, where the happiness of the client is always uppermost in mind, the more important the retiree has been to its success, the more important it is for the retiree—if out of sheer perverseness she insists on not dying—to just fade away like an old general without leaving even a ripple. Well, a healthy ego needs to leave a ripple. The inscribed watch and farewell parties can never take the place of a real honest-to-God ripple.

I was due to be put out to graze in February 1973 although only nine months before I'd been honored as Advertising Woman of Distinction by the Ad Club of Metropolitan Washington, D.C. In '67 I'd been unanimously elected national Advertising Woman of the Year. In the last few years two of my commercials had won "firsts" at the International Film Festivals in Cannes and Venice. Could I suddenly have started deteriorating all that fast? Physically I felt great. Couldn't remember when I'd had to stay home for even a cold. Professionally, I was never better. My mind was quicker, more incisive and nothing, almost nothing, could happen in the market place that I hadn't experienced in one form or another and successfully worked out.

There's a theory around—and this may account for the decreasing number of people engaged in the craft of advertising—that in order to make it as a copywriter or art director you have to be young and brash. But to be young and brash is not enough. To be old and experienced is not enough either. To be bright, talented, and open-minded, that's enough at any age because chances are, if you're young and bright, you get older and brighter and if you're young and brash, you just get older and brasher. As some bright old fellow once said, "You can teach techniques but you can't teach imagination." Besides, I've never believed that the earth is flat and that by the time you're fifty you get to the edge and fall over. So I was not about to apologize for my age. If the executives were lucky, they'd get to be a year older each year too.

But that kind of rationalization those last three years at Foote, Cone didn't do anything much to lift my depression. Nor did it help any to know that I was still receiving offers of employment from outside companies. Not as often as I used to, it's true. In the 1960s I considered it a lost fortnight if I hadn't received at least one great offer from another advertising agency or manufacturer. But the habit of loyalty to Foote, Cone was strong, and to the products I had mothered, even stronger. And the habit of minding, ingrained in my youth, was still very compelling. One of

the last things George had said to me before he died was ". . .
and I want you to stay with Foote, Cone & Belding." (This was
the height of the Revlon and Alberto-Culver offers.) "They'll
watch over you and protect you." And they did. However, in
twenty years there are bound to be change-overs in the top
echelons and the new executives, some from the outside, rarely
have the warm understanding or full feeling of closeness engen-
dered during the struggle and the heyday.

George was right about the protectiveness of Foote, Cone as he
was right about so many things. As I have indicated before, when
he was alive I held my salary down rather than make more money
than he did. He never knew that because I wouldn't have wanted
him to know that. Though I loved my work, I was always more
interested in being a woman first and an advertising person second.
When he died, Foote, Cone, without any prompting from me,
doubled my salary so I wouldn't have to change my way of living.
Then a few years later they doubled it again. This time, I guess,
because I was earning it. And for many years I was the highest-
salaried employee, male or female, in what was then the seventh
largest advertising agency in the world. With it went the appropriate titles: Senior Vice-President, Chairman of the Creative Board,
New York office, and I was the first woman appointed to the
Advertising Board of Directors. I am prepared to admit, however, that I was lucky and that all this is rare: most females in
business or industry are paid considerably less than males for the
same skills and talents and are accorded less recognition and,
despite the best efforts of women's lib, this wholly unfair situation
still continues today.

Foote, Cone was protective too when I was slapped with a suit
for $8 or $9 million (I don't remember which but what's a million
more or less when you're talking about that kind of money, especially when you don't have it?), along with some thirty other
recognized advertising executives and agency owners, for running
an ad in the New York *Times* protesting the kind of advertising
that the Patrolmen's Benevolent Association was using in its
campaign against the election of a civilian police review board.
One of their ads, I remember, showed a young, attractive, somewhat apprehensive white woman in a white coat coming out of a
subway entrance. It was nighttime and the street was dark and

deserted. The caption read: "The Civilian Review Board must be stopped. Her life . . . your life . . . may depend on it. . . ." And the text pitched the notion that a policeman might very well hesitate to rush to her (or your) aid because of the possibility of unjust censure by the police review board. That moment of hesitation, as he thought twice about the threat to his job and pension, could easily cost many lives.

To me the ads were an indictment of all policemen as individuals. The copy and illustration seemed excessive and designed to further exploit the racist fears that existed among middle-class whites. I resent advertising being used that way and was happy to lend my name to an ad decrying "the use of deceptive, inflammatory statements that confuse and frighten the public and make reasoned judgment difficult." I don't even approve of advertising agencies marketing political candidates like a cake of soap. Eisenhower in a cardigan sweater, looking like everybody's grandfather and talking over a bag of groceries, might be a timely political image in these days of inflation but seemed over-folksy fakery in the 1950s.

Our fine ad, however, did nothing to change the situation. The anti-review board ads won the election but the advertising agency that prepared the ads and instigated the suit didn't come out so well. The case was settled very low or dropped. At least I never heard of it again. Foote, Cone took it over on my behalf and handled it completely, with tact, sympathy, and never a word of reproof. There's a fantasy quality about being sued for several million dollars when you don't have even one. It's frightening, yet exhilarating; could all this be happening to a little girl from Brooklyn?

Yes, as I said, George was right about a lot of things. I don't remember ever winning a bet from him when he was alive. And we were always betting about everything. Whether it was a fact, a figure, a historical event, the pronunciation of a word, a baseball score, I was always awfully sure but awfully wrong. Even when he said, in one of his imitations of that great old scholar-detective Philo Vance, who smoked interminably something called a Régie cigarette as he made his pronunciamentos, "If you will look on the second line of the third paragraph in Volume V, you will find that fact adequately described," it seems to me now that we always did find the disputed fact adequately described on the second line of the third paragraph of Volume V. However, there was one bet I did win, although he wasn't around for me to collect, and that was the one when he said, "You're the type who should be married. I bet you'll be married within four months after I'm gone. And that's a thought that makes me happy." I'm glad it made him happy but that was fourteen years ago. The statute of limitations has long since run out on that bet.

Now, ten years after his death, I was again faced with the fact that I had not only lost my betting partner, I'd lost my bed partner, my tennis partner, my skiing partner, my battling partner, my dinner partner, my dancing partner, my mental companion, my traveling companion, my theater companion, my movie companion. But at that time I still had my children, my friends, my job! Now my children were married and living in other parts of the country and I was about to *not* have my job. My job that I loved with all its excitements and challenges and heartaches and gratifications. My job with all its problems and solutions and stimulating daily contacts.

What would I do with the time? I began to plan. I could sleep late mornings. I hate to sleep late mornings. It eats up the day. What's more, I don't need much sleep; six hours, maybe even seven after a really hard day. I had tried it all ways. Go to sleep at ten, wake up at four. Go to sleep at two, wake up at seven, even on a holiday. The only time I ever craved more sleep was when I had an early morning appointment with a client I was reluctant to face or a clothes closet that absolutely had to be cleaned out without further delay. Two-day weekends at home were just enough for me. Three-day holidays, unless I was away, left me bored, depressed, and turned in on myself. T.V. has never been much of an answer for me so if after an early morning walk I came home and read—and I'm addicted to reading—I'd get so engrossed in my book I'd forget to eat and notice the hour until suddenly it would be four in the morning with a full day ahead. Long ago I had discovered that, no matter how much one enjoys reading, it's much more delicious when there's someone else in the room you care about who's reading too. What might otherwise be loneliness becomes a cozy, pervading sense of shared peace.

So maybe a car. A car in the city? What a nuisance. Not only frightfully expensive to garage and insure but the battery's always dead by the time you get around to using it. After George died, I got rid of the car to the great relief of the doorman, who preferred Cadillacs and Lincolns to vintage cars with rumble seats parked near his fancy Park Avenue canopy. I figured I could always hire a car till I found out that in the city this requires advance planning and I'm not much of an advance planner. So I'd find myself alone since most of my friends have weekend homes. I remember one Sunday I went to a Kafka movie at twelve, then across the street to a Hollywood rerun at two, had a plate of cabbage soup complete with piroschki at the Russian Tea Room at four, made an off-Broadway play at six that let out around nine, then topped off the day with another movie, *I Am Curious Yellow*, which left me feeling blue and bleak. And broke, I hasten to add.

What about traveling? Alone? I'd tried that. I can make myself understood in only one language. (That's not quite true: by raising my voice several decibels, gesticulating broadly, and repeating one of the five Yiddish phrases I know, I have sometimes managed in Vienna, Rome, and would you believe Trinidad?) I could walk all over Copenhagen, Venice, Paris, Athens happy with just seeing and being there, but I found it impossible to face dinner alone in a foreign restaurant or to walk into a ship's bar in the evening by myself for a before-dinner cocktail. This was a devastating contrast to the Walter Mitty-esque dreams in which I had always pictured myself as walking into a room "poised, gracious, infinitely cool and in control of the situation."

The nadir of my solitary travels had been a three-day stopover in Belgrade. I had just enjoyed a most *gemütlich* week in Vienna with my friend Hilda. Now she was going on to visit Austrian relatives. The Foote, Cone office in Milan was expecting me in a few days and, since a way to get from Vienna to Milan was over Yugoslavia, I thought I'd take the opportunity to tour Dubrovnik on the Yugoslavian coast line, which I'd heard was even lovelier than the French or Italian Riviera. Because it was the height of the season, I could get no direct transportation to Dubrovnik. "Let me book you into Belgrade," said the Viennese agent. "From Belgrade it is an easy hitch to Dubrovnik. They have a new hotel in Belgrade. Just a little away from the heart of the city. Right on the river. Very luxurious. You will like it, I promise you. It is *très* American."

The brand-new *très* American hotel turned out to be a strange amalgam of conspicuous capitalist consumption and proletarian austerity. Downstairs, it was Miami Beach baroque, all velvet with crystal chandeliers. Upstairs, it was spartan institutional— long narrow halls off which opened identical rows of severely un- adorned cells, each one hardly wider than its narrow cotlike bed. As Henny Youngman would say, "When you put your key in the lock, it cut off the cross ventilation." (I could picture him on the phone: "Hello, room service? Send me up a room.")

Soon as I got to Belgrade, the concierge informed me, "Du- brovnik is full up. Full up with American hip-pees." By no means could he get me to Dubrovnik and, if he could, I'd have nowhere to sleep. He suggested that I stay with them instead and enjoy "beautiful" Belgrade. I resigned myself to four days in "beautiful" Belgrade. I knew no one, had no possible way of communicating when I walked into town, and was both oppressed and depressed by the unrelenting drabness of the weather, the architecture, and the people. Definitely not a tourist mecca.

Maybe beauty is in the eye of the beholder and I was just not in the proper mood to be alone. There were other guests in the hotel, mostly businessmen, it seemed, and I wished I could encourage a conversation but I was suddenly so shy, the corners of my mouth turned down in frozen silence and I put on, I'm sure, what George used to call my "trying-on-a-hat hauteur."

There was one particularly attractive English-speaking man, a West German executive type, who was brave enough to strike up a conversation. When he found out I was a businesswoman he wanted to show me his company brochures—a new twist on the old etchings? I resisted the idea but accepted his dinner invitation and suggested he bring along his brochures. He forgot them. Dinner was delightful, the food surprisingly good, the wine de- licious, the atmosphere romantic. We laughed a lot and lingered over the final nightcap. He asked me if he could walk me to my door, which turned out to be right next door to his. (Hotel room clerks are incurable matchmakers.) I quickly said, "Thank you and good night," and turned the lock. He spent the next few hours till dawn alternately trying to knock down the door—but softly—that separated our cells and importuning me on the telephone to examine his brochures. I don't know what sybaritic delights could have been stimulated by those pamphlets but I do know that, unlike the girl in the musical *Oklahoma* who cain't say no, I discovered I didn't know how to say yes.

On that same trip I also discovered how much I hated the business of seeing to my own luggage and that without someone to keep reminding me, "Notice how I'm not saying we'll miss the plane if we don't hurry," I'd arrive at each airport panting and anxious, at least three hours too early. All things considered, not the least of which was expense (heavy taxes and the stock market having decreased considerably the extra capital I'd need to maintain my way of life when the *fardeening* was finished), traveling alone was not an answer for me.

What kind of options were there for a woman in my position? And what about all the other women, or men either for that matter, who aren't in my position, who never earned what I make, who don't have a retirement fund to draw on? Most salaries, even in families with two incomes, don't allow for significant savings, and even those who were able to stash away a nest egg of a few stocks can hardly be drawing much sustenance from those stocks in today's depressed market. Certainly Social Security, on which most retired people depend exclusively for their income, has failed to keep pace with inflation and barely covers rent and food. If Social Security *is* insurance, why shouldn't widows collect double if—when the husband was alive—they both worked and paid? As for me, though I'd been contributing my share to the government since Congress first enacted the law and George had paid since they "let in" lawyers, I could count on nothing in return until I was seventy-two.

And I was luckier than most. I realized that. I know that the large majority of my contemporaries have almost no options at all as to what to do with their new leisure, except worry. However, this knowledge did not provide me with any solutions.

A publishing company suggested I write a book. I didn't think advertising writing necessarily led to good literature. My training had all been in the direction of maximum compression—get it all into about sixty characters on five lines or twenty-eight seconds for T.V. There was one copywriter, however, that I knew of, who had managed the successful transition to book-length writing and that was Joseph Heller, and his style could hardly be characterized as terse. His social conversation was another matter. A few years back, I had met him at a cocktail party.

"Your name is familiar. Polykoff. You're in advertising."

"How do you know?"

"Because I once wrote you a letter asking for a job."

"You did?"

"But you didn't give me a job. Even though I'm Jewish."

"I can't go around giving everyone a job who's Jewish."

"But you could have given me one."

"No, I couldn't."

"Why?"

"Because you're a man. And I only hire woman writers." That was the catch.

Later in the evening he offered to take me home—to Park Avenue and 62nd Street.

"I don't live on Park and 62nd Street," I protested. "I live on Park and 82nd."

"I can only take you to Park and 62nd."

"How come?"

"That's where I'm meeting my wife." That was *his* catch.

"So go meet your wife," I said. "Someone else will take me to Park and 82nd."

"That's not a nice attitude," he said. "First you don't give me a job. Now you don't let me take you home."

A person could go crazy writing dialogue like that but not Joe Heller. His is a formidable talent. My abilities were limited to writing copy so I told the publisher, "No, thanks." And I proposed to Foote, Cone that I use the next three years doing special projects which might attract new business for them.

To be innovative in advertising, you have to keep pushing yourself. At the ripe old age of twenty-six I had vowed to George on my birthday that no new generation would ever catch me asleep at the techniques. And I think my record reflects that. All the campaigns were quite startling in their day. We were one of the first to substitute people-talk for the pitchman-talk still prevalent in the 1950s. And in the 1960s, I gave them—*ta-ta!*—a commercial in four acts.

This sounds like an interminable commercial but it actually was a way of cutting down commercial clutter and repetition over the course of an hour television special, reducing the usual twelve thirty-second messages to only four program interruptions.

Clairol was sponsoring its first sixty-minute program, a network documentary about the debutante ball tradition in America. They had four major products at that time, all haircolorings. Miss Clairol —to add color and cover gray; Lady Clairol—to take out color and blonde the hair; Loving Care—to cover gray without changing the natural color; and Silk & Silver—to shine up and highlight gray. Each product had its own group of sixty-second commercials. When viewed alone, they were great. When viewed consecutively within the hour format, they were fatal to each other. Written always as though each product existed alone in the market, they canceled each other out back to back.

First I thought we could surmount this problem by writing new commercials in which each product would be assigned to a different age segment of the population. We were allotted six minutes of commercial time, which meant six interruptions of the program. I wanted maximum impact for each "sell" so my second thought was to eliminate two of these breaks by having each commercial run a minute and a half. An extra half minute would give me the additional time needed to build up an aura of acceptance for the product, to tone down hucksterism, diminish viewer irritation, and thus endear us to the consumer. (This may sound like madness in the light of today's T.V. viewing when gaggles of thirty-second commercials are permitted to crowd each other out of the viewers' consciousness. Even today, I believe in sixties for certain products. For my kind of copy, impact has always triumphed over numbers.)

Now I had these four expanded time slots in which to sell four haircoloring products to four different age groups which, I suddenly realized, occur naturally in a family. I saw a play like Thornton Wilder's *Our Town* with the spotlight shifting from generation to generation; each generation representative of one of my products. I could write the four one-and-a-half-minute commercials as if they were four acts of a six-minute play.

The other programs we were sponsoring were holiday specials. Why not have the whole family come together to one home for a holiday visit? Grandma, or the supermom, for Silk & Silver; her younger sister for Loving Care; oldest daughter, with two children, for a typical Miss Clairol mother and child; and Lady Clairol for the youngest daughter, who would be pictured as a blonde. *The Adams Family.*

I sent for a copy of *Our Town* and read it several times to capture the warmth and folksy quality of the original. The first time we ran *The Adams Family*, it had Roger Pryor as the voice over, but for all the subsequent readings Bing Crosby took over. His voice had just the right schmaltzy tones when he crooned the opening lines. This is the script for the opening (introductory) act.

FOOTE, CONE & BELDING	CLX-T-400
CLIENT: CLAIROL, INC.	"AS FILMED"
COPY FOR: TV SPECTACULAR	1/15/62

VIDEO	AUDIO
	(MUSIC UP AND UNDER) NARRATOR V.O.
1. FADE UP HI-WIDE SHOT OF ATTRACTIVE RESIDENTIAL AREA. CAMERA MOVES IN SLOWLY AROUND THE CORNER IN LONG SHOT TO THE ADAMS HOUSE.	1. This is a Clairol story about some nice people named Adams. You may know the family. . . .
LIGHTS GO ON SEPARATELY IN TWO UPSTAIRS BEDROOMS . . . KITCHEN ON STREET FLOOR AT LEFT . . . LIVING ROOM AT RIGHT.	Their house always looks so nice, so well cared for. . . . Let's go in. . . .
2. CAMERA COMES IN THROUGH BACK WINDOW. . . . WE SEE TWO WOMEN . . .	2. *Every*body comes in through the kitchen. The lady with the beautiful silvery hair.

VIDEO	AUDIO
WORKING ON LARGE CAKE AND LARGE-SIZED CUP CAKE . . . AT A CENTER TABLE IN KITCHEN.	That's Jane Adams. It's her birthday tonight.
CONNIE JOINS JANE	And that's her sister-in-law, Connie. She helped bake the cake. Connie looks good too. Her hair's so much prettier lately.
CONNIE MOVES TO WINDOW.	
3. CAMERA PANS UP AND DISSOLVES INTO SALLY'S ROOM. FATHER, LARRY, SALLY'S BABY.	3. Now let's go upstairs. (PAUSE)
4. FOLLOW SALLY TO CRIB.	4. Up here's Jane's daughter, Sally. She's come for the weekend with her husband and kids. Thirty-three years ago, she was the baby in that same crib. Real pretty, isn't she?
5. SALLY MOVES OUT VIEW INTO LAURIE'S ROOM VERY MESSED UP . . . SHE'S TALKING ON PHONE	5. And here's Laurie. She's a fine girl, too . . . even if her room could look a little neater. You know, she wasn't always a blonde. That's her picture when she graduated.
MOVE INTO MCU	Her young man's on the

VIDEO	AUDIO
	phone. He'll be meeting the whole family tonight. . . .
6. CUT TO CU	6. *LAURIE INTO PHONE— SOUND* ". . . don't be silly, darling, they'll be crazy about you." (Kiss.)
7. DISSOLVE TO LIVING ROOM. ONE OF THE WOMEN CALLS MAN TO HELP. CAMERA PULLS BACK AND ACTION CONTINUES UNTIL . . .	7. NARRATOR V.O. And here's Dick and John. They're married to the gals we met in the kitchen. Now we don't get to see too much of the men in a Clairol story, but their *good opinion* is plenty important. And *that's* the wonderful thing about *all Clairol haircolorings*. . . .
9. DISSOLVE TO 2 SHOT LAURIE AND SALLY	9. They get approval on every count!
10. CUT TO CU LAURIE'S HAIR, SUPER "LADY CLAIROL."	10. Laurie lightens her hair with ULTRA-BLUE LADY CLAIROL. She says it's a softer-looking, *dreamier* blonde.

VIDEO	AUDIO
11. CUT TO CU SALLY'S HAIR SUPER "MISS CLAIROL."	11. Sally uses MISS CLAIROL because . . . well, what could look more natural!
12. DISSOLVES INTO CLOSE-UP OF CONNIE IN KITCHEN. SUPER "LOVING CARE"	12. LOVING CARE washes away the gray in Connie's hair without changing her natural hair color.
13. JANE ADAMS HAS WALKED OVER TO PANTRY THAT HAS NO LIGHT IN IT. KITCHEN LIGHT ILLUMINES HER HAIR. SUPER "SILK & SILVER" LIGHT EFFECT.	13. CLAIROL SILK & SILVER makes gray hair shine . . . say, Jane's hair seems to shine even in the dark!
14. SLOW DISSOLVE OUT TO DARK SCREEN . . . OUTSIDE OF HOUSE.	14. We'll be back in a little while with more of the Clairol story about a nice family named Adams.

The expense for filming seemed prohibitive in those days, about $97,000. But I found a way to write it so that when the extra half minute was lopped off at the beginning of each commercial the remaining segments became perfect sixty-second spots for use alone and could run independently of *The Adams Family*. (Two segments of this won the Venice Cup at the International Film Festival that year.)

Variety reviewed it as "the first commercial ever aired that the program will interrupt . . . relative to most commercials, this one is cast like a Tolstoy novel."

We even ran an advertisement for the commercial in the New York *Times* inviting the public to tune in not to the program but to "The Clairol Story about the Adams Family" with the exact time when each one-and-a-half-minute act would be on the tube. Screen credits were listed for the writer, producer, director. Some T.V. columnists even reviewed it as if it were a dramatic presentation in itself.

Since then, there had been other challenges and other successful campaigns that reaffirmed my feeling that I was still making progress rather than atrophying on the vine.

The urge for self-improvement has been a vital force in me all my life. Six weeks after my first daughter was born I enrolled in a beauty school that prescribed hour after hour of exercises daily along with six tablespoons of mineral oil, eight oranges (peel and all), half a dozen kelp crackers that tasted like cardboard (no other food allowed that first week), and a rubber face patter to stimulate circulation so the face wouldn't fall when the weight did. My father, who was visiting with us at the time, observed me beating myself about the brow and chin and protested, "You call this self-improvement? This is what Hitler did to the Jews." I've often recalled that remark when I've been sweating it out in a sauna—the line between torment and self-improvement is a slim one indeed.

Then there was the time I changed my voice. Shortly after George died, the wife of one of his partners felt obliged to let me know as gently as possible that what stood between me and a successful career was my Brooklyn accent. The advertising business was a WASP business, she said, and regardless of how nice my associates might be to my face, after hours in their Connecticut homes and country clubs I would be a pariah and would be left in my deserted office, talking to myself in nasal Brooklyn tones. Forgetting that I already had what might be called a successful career, I panicked at the thought of my barren professional and social horizons and hied myself over to the Dixon School of Speech, which prided itself on being able to remove one accent and replace it with another of your choice. The accent I chose was a cross between Harvard and Abercrombie & Fitch. "That ought to do it," I thought.

First we had to lower my voice from the nasal passages to the diaphragm. This was accomplished by taking a deep breath, holding in the mid-section, and thinking down. As the breath was expelled, I was instructed to chant, "WHA . . . WHAY . . . WHEE . . . WHAU . . . WHOE . . . WHOO. WHA . . . WHAY . . . WHEE . . . WHAU . . . WHOE . . . WHOO." The children, hearing me in my bathroom practicing my "WHA . . . WHAY . . . WHEE . . . WHAU . . . WHOE . . . WHOO," thought I'd finally gone over the edge. For hours, in front of the mirror, I would read aloud, changing my ahs to rrrrs, my oi's to eye's, aw's to ah's, until I changed myself into such a fair lady that only my speech therapist knew for sure.

The next speech that I was called upon to make presented me with an opportunity to show off the new me. I invited about ten executives from Foote, Cone and Clairol as well as my husband's partner's wife. The speech went off extremely well—no Brooklyn spoken here. When it was over, the partner's wife was thrilled with the transformation her suggestion had wrought but Bill Wirth, one of my friends at Foote, Cone, took me aside and said, "It was a fine speech but I missed something."

"What?"

"*Our* Shirley."

In subsequent years I traveled across America and Europe giving speeches at various advertising colloquiums and I discovered that, up to a point, the more Brooklyn I let back in the better the audience reaction. I could tell by the number of people who came up to talk to me after the speech was over. I won't say the training was for nothing, however, because it did help me to conduct myself with more confidence and poise without compromising the emotional communication. And you should see the service I get at Abercrombie & Fitch!

So here I was self-improved, experienced, full of energy and good health, looking ahead to an abrupt termination of all my customary outlets. What is the use of knowing that you're the best you can make of yourself if it's to no avail? As a matter of fact, it wasn't to no avail. It inspired the next big Clairol campaign.

The "Does she . . . or doesn't she?" ads had been running for about eighteen years. The times had changed and it was time for a change. Women were no longer so concerned with what they were doing with their hair but rather with what they were doing with their lives. In view of the new emphasis on women as active, involved, multifaceted human beings, I felt it necessary to shift the accent away from haircoloring as an end in itself and to underscore instead the idea that haircoloring was simply one other aspect of a woman's commitment to develop her own potential to the fullest. In other words, here was self-improvement carried to a logical conclusion: "To know you're the best you can be!" The illustrations showed women in various professional roles —architect, lawyer, teacher, pilot, politician, instead of just mother and child (although a number of women we depict are shown having both children and careers).

"To know you're the best you can be" really caught on as a slogan and as a song. And if I felt that way about myself too, I decided, I'd just better figure out some long-range plan whereby I could translate this conviction into action. I had, from time to time, imagined that I would continue to keep myself alive and alert by serving as a consultant to businesses and agencies after I retired, but the prospect of working alone in a corner of my apartment didn't exactly excite me.

Then another idea began to intrude itself. As a result of a pitch for a major airline account, reputed to have a $20 million budget for advertising, the work I did brought Foote, Cone a fee of about $150,000. Bill Wirth, who was now head of the New York office, suggested that, at those rates, it might be profitable to incorporate me as a separate creative arm of the company with sufficient independent status to exclude me from the mandatory retirement policy governing regular employees. This was the first time that I seriously entertained the idea of going into business for myself. And perhaps the idea didn't seem so frightening since it still involved being under the protective umbrella of Foote, Cone.

The next time was when the Chicago office needed a special campaign for a Kimberly-Clark product that would be competitive with one of the products the agency already handled. This further reinforced the idea that I could be of use to Foote, Cone if I were set up in an autonomous company—a creative boutique that would be available whenever a conflict of interest arose.

The third time was when a giant rent-a-car outfit wanted creative only without the usual marketing, research, and media placement of a full-service agency.

The fourth time involved an even more daring variation. The notion that I consider opening a full-service agency all on my own with a $7 million airline account as my first client. The only other time such a startling undertaking had ever been suggested to me was when Larry Gelb of Clairol proposed that Frank Mayers and I take their $35 million advertising budget and set up our own agency. Though I know that's how most agencies get started, I felt it was out of the question then because of my loyalty to Foote, Cone. I still felt exactly the same way. With a difference. I saw the possibilities in having a company of my own that *wouldn't* necessarily be competitive.

I didn't pursue the airline offer but nonetheless the die was cast. The more I thought about having an agency of my own, the better I felt. The better I felt, the more frightened I got. Soon I wasn't sleeping at all. The question kept begging itself; could a little (retirement age) girl from Brooklyn find happiness and contentment as the head of her own company on Madison Avenue? The clincher came from Memphis when the Plough Company (Maybelline) asked me to compete against five or six other agencies for the launching of a new line of make-up. Because of a conflict with Clairol Cosmetics, then handled by Foote, Cone, the only way I could compete was as a totally separate company. Thus was born what is now Shirley Polykoff Advertising, Inc.

(P.S. We got the account.)

9

She Still Does!

—But not without further ado. We were still at Foote, Cone when I received a long-distance call from Harry Solmson, president of the Plough Company. Yes, we practically had their account but there was one formality they hadn't mentioned. Before a contract could be signed, there would have to be an interview with Mr. Plough. Could Ray Betuel and I meet with them in New York on the following Tuesday at six-thirty? They would be staying at the Barclay Hotel on Lexington and Forty-eighth.

I rushed to Ray's office. Over the years, he had been the head art director on most of my Foote, Cone assignments. If we did go into business (and I still wasn't sure I wanted to even though we already had one client and two other contracts ready for signing), we would go in together, he as the art director and I as the writer. In some agencies the writers and art directors team up and fight out the ideas in concert but I've always been something of a solo performer and so was Ray. We were both perfectionists and very respectful of each other's abilities, which was good. We quickly caught each other's ideas without too much explanation, which was even better. But best of all was the way our dispositions meshed. He was tough in the office with himself and his staff where I was tough only with myself, milk-toasty with the staff. He was a doll with the clients, never rattled, always good-humored, where I was highly volatile.

We had heard a lot about "old" Abe Plough and his disconcerting interviews and it didn't help matters much that I finished my work that day by four-thirty. I now had two hours to wait around and practice being sweetly reasonable. Outside, it was pouring rain and the Barclay was too close to our offices for a taxi but far enough away for us to get thoroughly soaked.

We met Mr. Plough with Mr. Solmson and Mr. Jenkins, their executive V.P., at their suite. Mr. Plough was a vigorous-looking man of about eighty-two with a polished apple face, shrewd eyes, and a hearing aid suspended from each ear. He sat down in the chair facing me.

"Young lady," he said, looking me straight in the eye, "why should we give you our business?"

I was a little startled. "Because we're awfully good," I said, "probably the best in the field."

"How do we know that?"

I hesitated. "You could just ask around."

"Do you have any other clients?"

"Yes, we have a perfume account and two yearly retainers about to be signed." I picked up the large brown envelope I had brought along. It contained all our contracts, my special agreements with Foote, Cone, maybe even my will. I riffled through the papers and pulled out a memo listing our account prospects, the agreed fees and all, and would have shown it to him but he jumped the gun.

"How much are the others paying you?"

I put the papers back. "I don't see how that's pertinent." Then, warming to the subject, I looked him straight in the eye and laughed. "In fact, I think that's very impertinent."

I thought I saw an answering gleam in his eyes but he turned to Ray and from then on it was as though I wasn't in the room. He spoke about me in the third person.

"Why doesn't she retire?" he asked Ray.

"Why don't *you* retire?" I butted in. It was as if I hadn't spoken.

"Are you married?" he asked Ray.

"Yes."

"Doesn't your wife object to your working with her"—he nodded in my direction—"all day?"

"Jesus Christ!" I said under my breath. But Ray was not to be ruffled: "No. As a matter of fact Gloria likes her very much."

"What will you do if she suddenly flies off to the Riviera and decides she likes it better there?"

"Well, we'd move our offices to the beach," Ray laughed.

"I hate sand," I said to no one in particular.

"She's just like me," Mr. Plough observed to Ray after a while.

"Are you sure your company can stand two of us?" I inquired sweetly.

It was still raining and it was already dark when we came out on the street again. We were almost back at the Foote, Cone offices when I noticed that the large brown envelope was empty. "Oh, my God, Ray," I said, "I've lost all our contracts!"

"What do you mean? You have them in your envelope."

"No. I must have taken them out and left them in their suite. Look, Ray, you go on. I'll go back to the hotel!"

"Come on," he said, "we'll go back together."

We were almost at the Barclay when I spotted something white in the gutter. I darted between cars and scooped up a pile of dripping papers and hugged them to my breast. They had been run over several times but were, miraculously, still intact. (Is this any way to run a business?) They dried out fine, I erased the tire marks, and by next day they were as good as new.

We opened at the Drake Hotel to mixed reviews. We rented a two-room suite and hailed it as the new headquarters of Shirley Polykoff & Betuel, Inc. Ray, the art director, took over the bedroom, from which the beds had been removed, and installed the print production department (one paste-up man) near the window. The accounting department, which also doubled as traffic control, sat to the right of the production department so she could answer the telephone. Our T.V. head, a gentleman of discretion and tact, got the remaining corner of the bedroom which, as it happened, dominated the entrance to the bathroom, and since the lock on the door seldom worked, be became the relucant moderator of everyone's comings and goings. To make matters worse, storyboards and artwork were stored in the bathtub, so traffic could be especially heavy. In the living room, each of the two windows got its own art director. They were separated from me by a green damask sofa in front of which was a coffee table that more than fulfilled its function. Opposite me, next to the closet which housed our file system in grocery cartons, sat my secretary, while I occupied a stuffed armchair in front of a spindly period desk barely strong enough to hold my 1920 Remington (a typewriter that knows *I* would never dream of retiring *it* and rewards me accordingly). The conference room was the single bedroom opposite us which we hired for client meetings and presentations. Stretched across the bed, propped up against a couple of pillows, even the coolest campaign takes on an illicit intimacy.

"So this is where it's at," said one of our clients with unerring accuracy.

What started out to be temporary accommodations stretched out for a long year. We had only one phone number so hardly anyone could ever get through, and we were so busy servicing our clients there was never enough time in the day to look at suitable real estate. When Ray and I did get out with an agent, nothing we were shown seemed to have the right combination of convenience (I do my best thinking on foot, so I wanted it to be a walkable distance from my home), chic (we wanted an address that would sound as successful as we hoped to become), and the proper size (maybe a whole floor to ourselves with the elevator doors opening up on our reception room; and with space large enough to house our needs yet small enough to be affordable). We finally dismissed this want as wishful thinking. Everything we saw was either hopelessly vast or vastly hopeless. No light. No charm. No character.

We began with a select group of clients: Houbigant Perfumes, Kimberly-Clark's New Freedom, Miss Clairol from Bristol-Myers, and the new line of Maybelline make-up from Schering-Plough.

For Houbigant's Chantilly, we bought the song "He Touched Me" and let it build over a man-and-woman situation that climaxed with the line, "Touch her with Chantilly—and suddenly nothing is the same." For their other advertised fragrance, Musk, a younger scent with unisex appeal, we used "Wear it to provoke a primal response—the perfume with the power to persuade," thus identifying with the current passion for "primitive naturalness" that was sweeping the young market.

To potential users of New Freedom Feminine Pads by Kotex,

we held out the joys of complete mental and physical comfort with "For peace of mind and body. When you've got it you can forget it." "No pins. No belts. No doubts."

For Miss Clairol hair color, Natural Wear Formula, we inaugurated the new campaign "Does she . . . or doesn't she? She still does!"—showing clips from our old T.V. commercials juxtaposed against shots of the same models as they appear today, ten years later, still using the product. In addition we continued to celebrate the greater liberation of today's woman with "To know you're the best you can be!"

But the most fun was the cosmetics. That was the *real* challenge. The Plough Company had given us a fine line of make-up. The packaging was beautiful, the products were excellent, the price was right. But cosmetics are always difficult, especially today when what you can legally say circumscribes the promises you can make.

A good illustration—to keep it away from products we have—is, let's say, a pharmaceutical remedy. You can't say doctors approve of X brand, only that *some* doctors do (if they do), and then you have to be able to back that up with medical documentation. You can't say *relieves*, even if it actually does, only that it *helps* relieve. And you can't say that either unless you add "with constant use" or specify the number of hours you will get this *temporary* relief. Encumbered by these qualifying adjectives, which really don't change what actually gets through to the listener, the message sounds badly written and awkward. I think it's fine that companies should back up whatever claims they make with medical and laboratory affidavits and proofs of results. It's a very desirable form of consumer protection, but it can become a copywriter's nightmare. And that's what we're discussing here. And since *hope*, in relation to cosmetics, is a chief ingredient, you have to say what you want to in a way that's consonant with the advertising and FTC codes, with the personal predilections of the medical and legal staffs, and the idiosyncrasies of some young fellow over at the T.V. networks.

Again, in keeping with the times, we decided to understate, to keep the pitch honest, young and—cheeky! We came up with "Hello! Fresh Face. That's *you* with a little help from Maybelline," and put these words against some of the freshest, loveliest faces in the modeling business. The results in the test market from our print and television were so encouraging, the company committed itself to a national campaign without further testing and within the year had cornered a significant share of the market.

It was at one of the meetings with Maybelline in Memphis that I first noticed how pale and fragile my sturdy partner had begun to look. Something in Ray's face suddenly reminded me of the pain I used to see in George just before his illness had reached the acute stage. My heart literally stopped for a moment with an awful sense of foreboding. I pushed this to the back of my mind during the subsequent months but when we finally found the right office space, in July 1973, I do remember wondering if Ray would still be alive to enjoy it when it was ready for occupancy.

The new offices—we moved in that Christmas—were just what we had wanted and thought we could never achieve: a floor-through with elevators opening on our own reception room in a small smart building on the most elegant business street in town! East 57th Street between Madison and Park avenues. We partitioned the space to maximize light and cheer, chose the furniture on the same principle, designed the stationery, and ordered a hot neon sign for the cool crisp reception room: Shirley Polykoff & Betuel. (Ray thought it sounded more offbeat to leave his first name out.)

The neon sign arrived the day he was admitted to the hospital. He never saw it. On February 6, 1974, he died of cancer of the liver, the same way George had. I lost not only a marvelously imaginative and resourceful business partner but a friend I had worked with for almost twenty years.

During the next few months I fell apart but couldn't let it show. The responsibility of being in business for myself and for seven other people, who, in turn, were responsible for dependents of their own, struck me with terrible force. Ray and I had decided when we became employers that we would do all the things we had always wanted our employers to do for us in terms of pensions, life and health insurance, and salaries. Now I wasn't sure I could swing it alone: I, who had always been protected by a large organization like Foote, Cone & Belding, was now supposed to assume the protection of others while feeling totally vulnerable and unprotected myself. Sending the neon sign back to have the "& Betuel" cut off was one of the loneliest things I've ever had to do.

One of the strengths that helped keep me together was Gordon Kolvenbach, our television producer. In the midst of the maelstrom, he proved to be a source of sustenance at every juncture, transforming major dilemmas into minor problems, and coming up with sensible easy solutions to situations that seemed insurmountable to me (all this while turning out beautifully executed commercials). My secretary, Marilyn Robinson, who had been with me at Foote, Cone, also provided me with strong shoulders to lean on, and the rest of the staff rallied round me with such warmth and fellow feelings that I couldn't help but respond to treatment. And if it's true that every cloud, no matter how dark, has a silver lining, ours came in the form of Dick Huebner, whom I hired as our new art director and whose taste and artistic inventiveness are wonderfully matched by his pleasant manner and generous disposition.

This would be a good place to explain the key functions within any advertising agency, large or small, and it might be easiest for me to delineate them in terms of our own personnel. First you have to have an account of course. In large agencies, this is the function of new business groups, account executives, top officers who use their contacts, old school ties, and reputation of work done by the agency to open doors and sell, sell, sell. In a small group like ours, it's the reputation of the principals that brings in the clients.

There are now nine of us. Whenever we get a new account or start a new campaign, we all get together to extract the essence of the product, its uses and special benefits. After that we read all the research, pinpoint the market, and assess the competition (this is the "thinking out square" part, the strategy).

Then the writer (in our case, you get the senior writer, copy chief, and president all in one) works out the campaign theme, and starts to construct the headlines and copy in a way that will maximize the impact in the catchiest, shortest number of words (this is the "saying it with flair" part). Our two other writers get into the act here and contribute ideas of their own.

Enter the art director, Dick Huebner, and the second art director, Debbie Fritts. After a discussion, in which I can usually tell how they like the ideas by the look on their faces, rough layouts are started to suggest best ways to dramatize the idea in magazines. (Even if it's to be a television-only campaign, I have always found it sharpens the thinking to make print ads first. A good print ad is harder to do. It must bring the message out fast and clear so the point gets across even to read-as-you-run-ers.)

After the campaign has been worked on and worked over from every angle, the writers do a television script with indications on the left-hand side of the page as to what the cameraman should be photographing. Now we are ready to enlist the talents of the T.V. producer. Gordon Kolvenbach, who enjoys this title (but actually helps run the whole office—he's that kind of a guy), goes into a huddle with the rest of us. He and Dick immediately throw out my left-hand columns and substitute their own visualizations and effects. (Bearing in mind that I have the last word or almost, they occasionally allow me a concept or two.)

T.V. storyboards which look like giant comic strips are then drawn up and the art directors pencil in the pictures that dramatize the script. These will be used later for estimates and as guidelines in filming the commercial.

At this point the storyboards, print layouts, and general strategy are presented to the client for approval. This brings in the agency account person, and in our office this is Jane Blanchard, who has an inexhaustible supply of patience, efficiency, and finesse in serving as the interface between client and agency. In large full-service agencies there is also a media department that buys the scheduled T.V. time and print space, a group of research types and special marketers. Because in our office each of us came up the hard way, step by step, we are familiar with all these techniques and know where we can tap the experts should we need them; a most economical arrangement for the client.

After the client has okayed the campaign (this could take months and entail much heartache and nail biting on the part of certain copywriter/agency heads), the next step is to prepare the print ads in finished mechanical form for plate making. This involves a skilled "paste-up" person like Tony Rozenbergs, who sizes and positions the retouched illustration together with the message, which has already been designed and set into type by the art director, and the client's logo into an exact replica of what will appear in the magazines.

Meanwhile, back on the T.V. location, Gordon and Dick are orchestrating the director, photographer, models, and the announcer, whom they have hired with the approval of the client. In commercial television, just as in Hollywood, the cutting room is a critical juncture not only for screen effects but for pace, clarity, and professionalism. By now, of course, we've run into lots of big money which should, but sometimes doesn't, tally with our advance estimates. On these rare occasions nail biting escalates to hair pulling (our own and one another's) as we try to reconcile costs.

Recently we have been joined by my eldest daughter, Alix Nelson, formerly a senior editor in a publishing firm which she left in order to write her own articles and books and to help write copy for us. (She has been a source of inspiration and guidance in the writing of this book as well.) Businesses used to be planned to go from father to son. These days they may go from mother to daughter—perhaps even to granddaughters (my ten-year-old granddaughter, Corin, and thirteen-year-old, Shawn, do an impromptu critique of every T.V. commercial they see).

I've often been asked to address college and career seminars on how the novice breaks into the advertising field. Unfortunately it's not easy. (I suppose it helps to have a grandmother in the business.) In order to get your foot in the door you must have something to show other than your good intentions and your Bachelor of Arts degree. The most direct and persuasive approach for a writer is to write—take ads you don't like and rewrite them so you do. Paste them up neatly in a book showing your *improved* version and the ad that ran. This requires hard work, careful thought, shows you are self-motivating and ambitious, and is the only way I know to impress a possible employer. Your best strategy is to try to get into a small agency where you are forced to do a little of everything and quickly get the feel of the business as well as the experience. Another way is to get even the most menial job in the advertising office of a department store. Sooner or later, in an emergency, they'll give you a chance to write an ad. There is a unique advantage in retailing—you can tell by the sales figures on Saturday whether the ad you wrote the previous Monday pulled, and how well.

But the time-honored way of moving into advertising, although it may be a dead end for a woman in other fields, is to enter at the level of secretary in the department in which you wish to advance. I know more than a dozen former secretaries who are now copywriters, television producers, and account executives. Art directing requires special art training of some kind and entry-level jobs usually occur in the paste-up department.

One of the toughest parts of running your own company (should you happen to get that far) is knowing that whatever you do or say has consequences for the entire agency from which no one can protect you. At Foote, Cone, I could afford to say whatever I honestly believed to the clients—that was part of my value. If I overstepped in any way, account men and other members of the organization could intercede and mitigate, keep me in the closet for a week, then trot me out again all shiny and contrite. That way, my integrity was never in question (to me): I didn't have to leave anything unspoken that I thought was important for the client to hear.

Now I am caught in a conflict of conscience. If I'm adamant about a point on which the client and I differ, I run the risk of alienating precisely the person I'm trying to serve best. If I hold back and refrain from rocking the boat in order to keep relations harmonious, I feel guilty of limiting and compromising the very contribution I've been hired to make.

I keep seeing the image of my father with hand raised chasing me around the dining-room table while I insist on finishing the sentence. "Not another word," warns my father. "I don't care. It isn't right," I holler back as I duck and catch it.

I used to catch it in grade school too. "Not another word," the teacher says as she sticks a paster over my mouth. And as I continue to mumble behind the adhesive, she banishes me to the coat closet. Four hours later, when it's time to go home, I'm discovered, forgotten in the closet, hungry, silent, subdued at last. "Why didn't you speak up?" she scolds.

Either way, you can't win.

Looking back over a half century of my life in advertising (of course, I started in the cradle), I realize that in so many ways I *have* been a winner. Let me count the ways: I've achieved goals beyond those I set for myself; I've enjoyed the challenges of my

work and have never been bored; I've been a successful *fardeener*
—Momma, do you hear?; I've received public recognition to an
extent that still amazes me and have made friends that have en-
riched my life and proved in time of (my) need to be great
friends indeed. I've had the pleasures and the problems of a loving, close-knit family and now have the pride of being a grandmother of four. As I've always told my children, "Take the time to
be aware that you're happy when you're happy. Don't wait till
tomorrow to realize how happy you could have been yesterday."

Sometimes I'm so busy during the day that I have to take time
out at night from sleep to savor fully the joys and satisfactions of
what has been a most rewarding career. In fact, three extravagant
celebrations stand out in my mind that seem more like Cinderella
stories than true-to-life happenings. Except they did happen, and
to me.

One was Clairol's "Tribute to Shirley," which took place at the
St. Regis Hotel on the occasion of my official retirement from
Foote, Cone. Twenty-three men who had been closest to me in the
entire Foote, Cone/Clairol association—from charter member
Tom Hogan to the most recent, John O'Toole—assembled in
formal attire to participate in an evening's program designed to
highlight the more memorable incidents of our collaboration and
to express the full measure of their affection. It was a kind of "This
Is Your Life." It began by my being picked up at my home by
two handsome and distinguished escorts, Bill Wirth, and Don
Shea. They came complete with photographer and chauffered
Rolls-Royce. I was whisked away to the Watteau Suite, which consisted of separate cocktail and dining rooms, and according to the
chronicler of the occasion, "was greeted with a kiss by every man
in attendance," toasted with a rare vintage Dom Perignon champagne and a heavenly assortment of Beluga caviar and hors
d'oeuvres. Next came the presentation: there were eight black
cards, each approximately three feet high, propped up on chairs
around the walls of the drawing room. On the front of each card
in white letters were the most successful campaign headlines I'd
written, and listed on the backs of each was a gift for me from
either Clairol or Foote, Cone. They ranged from having my hair
done each week for the rest of my life at New York's best-known

hair-care specialists, The Private World of Leslie Blanchard, through a Maine Chance Day once a month at Elizabeth Arden, to the complete set of my new blonde office furniture from Foote, Cone (including my legendary 1920 Remington) as well as the latest in electronic visual and sound equipment for my new office. Not to forget the sterling silver Franklin Mint plate engraved on the front with the Miss Clairol mother and child and on the back with the signatures of all those present.

The dinner itself and the wines that went with it, like a 1961 red Château Creole ⚡64, were a coup even for the famous St. Regis cuisine. For dessert, Crêpes Suzette accompanied by a ⚡1 Bollinger Brut set the perfect mood for the generous testimonials by each man present. But the pièce de résistance was the personal gift from the three Gelbs. It was a huge gold pendant encrusted with magnificently faceted diamonds and suspended from a heavy Florentine gold chain. In size and splendor, it could have complimented the bosom of Catherine the Great. I felt great to have it compliment mine.

The photographer recorded every phase of the festivities for a memory book, but each moment remains so vivid, how could I possibly forget?

The second occasion was the time I was elected National Advertising Woman of the Year and received a beautiful Calder mobile from the Foote, Cone group ("All that money," said the president, "for about thirty-seven cents worth of tin?") and a Tiffany diamond and gold arrangement from Clairol. It was a huge gold chestnut with pavé diamond center designed by Schlumberger which could be worn as a discreet pin or a knock-'em-dead ring.

The third Cinderella time was when *Life* magazine asked me to be a spokeswoman for advertising at a four-day symposium, The Worlds We Live In, held in Ponte Verde, Florida, in 1964.

I was the only woman included with 180 men! And such men! The Honorable LeRoy Collins, on communications; His Excellency Hervé Alphand, then Ambassador of France to the United States, on diplomacy; the Reverend Billy Graham on religion; the distinguished James E. Webb, on aeronautics and space; Dr. James A. Perkins, president of Cornell University, on education; Leon-

ard Hall, former chairman of the Republican National Committee, on politics. On business, there were Grant Simmons,
president of the Simmons Company; John D. Mack, marketing
director of Clairol; and Edward L. Bond, president of Young &
Rubicam. These were just a few of the distinguished panel. And if
it sounds like I'm name-dropping it's only because I am. (It's
still hard for me to believe that I was included in such august
company.) To say nothing about all those beautiful men from
Life magazine.

It was like a heavenly dream. Before I went down to the conference I went to Bergdorf Goodman and picked out four super
evening gowns (elegant and understated—in everything but price)
plus a chic golf ensemble. I didn't know how to play golf but no
one seemed to notice. Since I was the only woman present I had a
retinue of men to accompany me to every activity—at timed in-
tervals during each day, flowers would arrive, the guard would
change, and we would march the few steps in unison to the next
event.

The last evening, they gave a special dinner dance in the out-
door patio. Just me in a lovely long gown dancing with 180 men.
Maybe that's what my family calls "a slight advertising exaggeration," but it did feel like I danced with all 180 of them.

It seems to me that everything that happens in my life is like an
echo—a reverberation from the past—of moments and meanings
that were decisive in shaping the direction of things to come.
Even something as apparently insignificant as the first speech I
ever made. I had told my mother that I was about to make my
first business address to an all-male group, and my mother said,
"Fine! I'm coming down to hear you."

I said, "You can't come, Momma. It's not like I'm graduating
from someplace. This is business."

"That's all right," she said, "I'll come down anyway." So we
compromised. And she came down. When the speech was finished,
the men stood up—there were about fifty of them—and to make
me feel good, I guess, they whistled and cheered. When I left the
auditorium with my mother, I said, "Well, Momma?" expecting
my gold star, and she said, "You know something, Shirley? That
was a nice proportion of men to women."

That's one woman's viewpoint—as is this book.

So let's close with a toast to what Shakespeare calls "the fair adventure of tomorrow." Or, to quote my favorite line from Marx (Groucho), "Hello! I must be going!"